WORLD SURVEY ON THE ROLE OF WOMEN IN DEVELOPMENT 2014

GENDER EQUALITY AND SUSTAINABLE DEVELOPMENT

United Nations Entity for Gender Equality
and the Empowerment of Women

CONTENTS

PREFACE

The immense social, economic and environmental consequences of climate change and loss of essential ecosystems are becoming clear. Their effects are already being felt in floods, droughts, and devastated landscapes and livelihoods. Among those most affected are women and girls, given the precariousness of their livelihoods, the burden of securing shelter, food, water and fuel that largely falls on them, and the constraints on their access to land and natural resources. As the global community grapples with the challenges of sustainable development and the definition of the Sustainable Development Goals, the *World Survey on the Role of Women in Development* 2014 asserts the central role of gender equality. It charts the rationale and actions necessary to achieve sustainable development.

Linking gender equality with sustainable development is important for several reasons. It is a moral and ethical imperative. Efforts to achieve a just and sustainable future cannot ignore the rights, dignity and capabilities of half the world's population. To be effective, policy actions for sustainability must redress the disproportionate impact on women and girls of economic, social and environmental shocks and stresses. Finally, women's knowledge, agency and collective action has huge potential to improve resource productivity, enhance ecosystem conservation and sustainable use of natural resources, and to create more sustainable, low-carbon food, energy, water and health systems. Failure to capitalize on this would be a missed opportunity. Women should not be viewed as victims, but as central actors in moving towards sustainability.

The *World Survey* does not attempt to cover the exceedingly wide range of aspects of sustainable development. It identifies a select range of issues that are fundamental to women's lives and are strategic for achieving gender equality and sustainability. It analyses patterns of growth, employment generation and the role of public goods; food production, distribution and consumption; population dynamics and women's bodily integrity; and water, sanitation and energy.

Three criteria are employed to assess the likelihood of policy actions achieving gender equality. Do they support women's capabilities and their enjoyment of rights? Do they reduce, rather than increase, women's unpaid care work? And do they embrace women's equal and meaningful participation as actors, leaders and decision-makers?

The *World Survey* 2014 is a serious and thoughtful contribution to our understanding of how gender equality relates to sustainable development. This is a resource that strengthens the hands of policy actors in different parts of the world – whether in government, civil society, international agencies, or the private sector. It is my firm hope that it will lead to policies and actions that enhance gender equality and the full enjoyment by women and girls of their human rights.

The *World Survey* will be presented to the General Assembly in October 2014.

Phumzile Mlambo-Ngcuka
Under-Secretary-General
and Executive Director, UN Women

ACKNOWLEDGMENTS

UN Women would like to thank a number of experts and representatives across the United Nations system for their inputs into *The World Survey on the Role of Women in Development 2014: Gender Equality and Sustainable Development*.

The contributing authors who developed background papers that formed the basis of the chapters of the publication include: Melissa Leach and Lyla Mehta, Institute of Development Studies, University of Sussex (United Kingdom); Elissa Braunstein, Colorado State University (United States); Sakiko Fukuda-Parr, The New School (United States); Elizabeth Hartmann, Anne Hendrixson and Jade Sasser, the Population and Development Program, Hampshire College (United States), and Isha Ray, Energy and Resources Group, University of California at Berkeley (United States).

In order to ensure that the *World Survey* reflected a balanced range of experiences and the diversity of policy, advocacy and research activities around gender equality and sustainable development, UN Women organized several consultations to receive guidance and input on the content of the report.

An initial brainstorm on the key issues in gender and sustainable development was organized jointly with the United Nations Research Institute for Social Development (UNRISD) in Geneva in May 2013 with a small group of experts. The attendees were Bina Agarwal, Institute of Economic Growth, University of Delhi and The University of Manchester (United Kingdom); Sarah Cook, UNRISD; Wendy Harcourt, International Institute of Social Studies, Erasmus University (the Netherlands); Melissa Leach; and Anita Nayar, The Dag Hammarskjöld Foundation (formerly, United Nations Non-Governmental Liaison Service).

Subsequently, a two-day concepts and methods workshop was organized at UN Women headquarters in New York with presentations by experts on various key topics identified at the brainstorm. Participants at this workshop included Andrew Fischer, International Institute of Social Studies, Erasmus University (the Netherlands); Sakiko Fukuda-Parr; Elizabeth Hartmann; Anne Hendrixson; Melissa Leach; Michael Levien, John Hopkins University (United States); Anita Nayar; Isha Ray; Dianne Rocheleau, Clark University (United States); and Margarita Velasquez, Regional Centre for Multidisciplinary Research (Mexico).

An expert group meeting was organized jointly with the Food and Agriculture Organization of the United Nations (FAO) in Rome in late February 2014, to review and discuss the first drafts of the background papers, on the basis of which the authors made revisions for a second draft. Apart from the authors, the attendees included researchers and practitioners with expertise and experience on the different thematic areas covered: Denisse Cordova, FIAN International (Germany); Wendy Harcourt; Marjorie Mbilinyi, Tanzania Gender Networking Programme (Tanzania); Mohan Rao, Jawaharlal Nehru University (India); Liane Schalatek, Heinrich Böll Foundation North America (United States); Stephanie Seguino, University of Vermont (United States); and Simon Thuo, Global Water Partnership Eastern Africa (Uganda). Representatives from the United Nations system included Martina Otto, United Nations Environment Programme; Patricia Colbert and Jennifer Nyberg, World Food Programme; Solomon Asfaw, Chiara

Brunelli, Ida Christensen, Chiara Cirulli, Francesca Di Stefano, Carol Djeddah, Susan Kaaria, Eric Jesper Karlsson, Regina Laub, Leslie Lipper, Dominique Mortera, Ana Paula de la O Campos, Martha Osorio, Inna Punda, Terri Raney, Gina Seilern, Jomo Kwame Sundaram, and Rob Vos from FAO.

Through an extensive peer review process, a number of experts and United Nations technical staff provided substantive contributions and guided the finalization of the report. The peer reviewers included: Bina Agarwal, Carmen Diana Deere, University of Florida (United States); Jennie Dey De Pryck, Gender in Agriculture Partnership (Italy); Soma Dutta, ENERGIA Asia (India); Diane Elson, University of Essex (United Kingdom); Andrew Fischer, Wendy Harcourt, Jennifer Olmstead (United Nations Population Fund); Stephanie Seguino, Gita Sen, Bangalore Institute of Management (India); Dzodzi Tsikata, University of Ghana (Ghana); and Peter Utting, UNRISD.

At UN Women, the substantive work on the World Survey was coordinated by Shahrashoub Razavi and Seemin Qayum under the guidance of Saraswathi Menon and John Hendra. Somali Cerise and Laura Turquet made valuable contributions to finalize the text; Sophie Browne and Norberto Rodrigues undertook research assistance and fact-checking; and Talita Mattos provided administrative support. Comments on the chapters were provided by Ginette Azcona, Christine Brautigam, Sylvia Hordosch, Papa Seck and Silke Staab. The design and production was coordinated by Mika Mansukhani and Carlotta Aiello.

CHAPTER /1

ABOUT THE WORLD SURVEY ON THE ROLE
OF WOMEN IN DEVELOPMENT

The twin challenges of building pathways to sustainable development and achieving gender equality have never been more pressing. As the world moves towards the post-2015 development agenda, the present *World Survey* not only shows why each challenge is so important, but also why both challenges must be addressed together, in ways that fully realize the human rights of women and girls and help countries to make the transition to sustainable development.

Dominant patterns of production, consumption and distribution are heading in deeply unsustainable directions (see A/CONF.216/PC/7). Humanity has become a key driver of earth system processes and the overexploitation of natural resources, the loss of key habitats and biodiversity and the pollution of land, seas and the atmosphere are becoming increasingly evident. Scientific understandings are clarifying the huge economic, social and environmental challenges posed by such threats as climate change and the loss of essential ecosystem services, as humanity approaches or exceeds so-called "planetary boundaries" (Intergovernmental Panel on Climate Change, 2013; Rockström and others, 2009). Already, human interactions with the environment are producing unprecedented shocks and stresses, felt in floods, droughts and devastated urban and rural landscapes and livelihoods, while many people and places have suffered from a nexus of food, energy, environmental and financial crises. These unsustainable patterns add to poverty and inequality today, especially for the third of the world's population directly dependent on natural resources for their well-being, and create deep threats for future generations (Unmüßig, Sachs and Fatheuer, 2012).

The causes and underlying drivers of unsustainability and gender inequality are deeply interlocked

The effects of unsustainable patterns of development intensify gender inequality because women and girls are often disproportionately affected by economic, social and environmental shocks and stresses (Neumayer and Plümper, 2007). The causes and underlying drivers of unsustainability and of gender inequality are deeply interlocked. Both are produced by development models that support particular types of underregulated market-led growth and the persistence of unequal power relations between women and men (Wichterich, 2012). Such development patterns rely on and reproduce gender inequalities, exploiting women's labour and unpaid care work. The same development trajectories also produce environmental problems, as market actors seek and secure profit in ways that rely on the overexploitation of natural resources and the pollution of climates, land and oceans. Such market-led pathways are leading in directions that are unsustainable in social and ecological terms, and ultimately in economic ones too, undermining the conditions for future progress.

Growing international debate now highlights the need to move economies and societies onto more sustainable paths, whether to avert crisis and catastrophe, or enable prosperity through "green economies". Policy responses to date have not always emphasized that the realization of human rights must guide such efforts, or prioritized the need to address gender inequality. Also frequently missing in such debates is a sense of the trade-offs involved. Sustainability is often presented as if policy solutions were clear-cut. Yet many dilemmas arise: for instance between finance for different kinds of low-carbon energy; between prioritizing food or biofuels in land use; and between preserving forests to mitigate global climate change or to meet local livelihood needs, to name a few. In many instances, policy approaches that seek to promote sustainability or "green economy" goals can undermine women's rights and gender equality. How such dilemmas are addressed has profound implications for who gains and loses, both among social groups and between local, national and global interests.

Yet this is also a time of opportunity. There are many examples around the world of alternative development pathways that move towards sustainability with gender equality. Gender equality and sustainable development can reinforce each other in powerful ways (Agarwal, 2002; Buckingham-Hatfield, 2002; Cela, Dankelman and Stern, 2013; Johnsson-Latham, 2007).

A/ GENDER EQUALITY AND SUSTAINABLE DEVELOPMENT: SYNERGIES AND TENSIONS

The centrality of gender equality, women's empowerment and the realization of women's rights in achieving sustainable development has been increasingly recognized in recent decades. This recognition is evident in a number of international norms and agreements, including principle 20 of the Rio Declaration on Environment and Development,[1] adopted in 1992, in its statement regarding the full participation of women being essential to achieving sustainable development. In the Beijing Declaration and Platform for Action,[2] adopted by Member States in 1995, governments were called upon to integrate gender concerns and perspectives into policies and programmes for sustainable development. The centrality of gender equality has also been articulated in the outcome document of the United Nations Conference on Sustainable Development, entitled "The future we want", adopted in 2012, which included recognition of the importance of gender equality and women's empowerment across the three pillars of sustainable development, economic, social and environmental, and resolve to promote gender equality and women's full participation in sustainable development policies, programmes and decision-making at all levels (General Assembly resolution 66/288, annex).

Linking gender equality and sustainable development is important for several reasons. First, it is a moral and ethical imperative: achieving gender equality and realizing the human rights, dignity and capabilities of diverse groups of women is a central requirement of a just and sustainable world. Second, it is critical to redress the disproportionate impact of economic, social and environmental shocks and stresses on women and girls, which undermine the enjoyment of their human rights and their vital roles in sustaining their families and communities. Third, and most significantly, it is important to build up women's agency and capabilities to create better synergies between gender equality and sustainable development outcomes.

There is growing evidence of the synergies between gender equality, on the one hand, and economic, social and environmental sustainability, on the other. For example, when women have greater voice and participation in public administration, public resources are more likely to be allocated towards investments in human development priorities, including child health, nutrition and access to employment (Chattopadhyay and Duflo, 2004). Ensuring women's access to and control over agricultural assets and productive resources is important for achieving food security and sustainable livelihoods (Food and Agriculture Organization of the United Nations (FAO), 2011). Women's knowledge, agency and collective action are central to finding, demonstrating and building more economically, socially and environmentally sustainable pathways to manage local landscapes; adapt to climate change; produce and access food; and secure sustainable water, sanitation and energy services.

premised on maintaining gender inequalities, such as through maintaining gender wage gaps and entrenching gender discriminatory norms, values and institutions (Seguino, 2000; Kabeer and Natali, 2013).

Further, as governments and donor agencies increasingly target women as critical agents for community adaptation to climate change; in their role as smallholders as the mainstay of sustainable food production; and through limiting their reproductive rights as the answer to population-environment problems; there is a danger of entrenching gender stereotypes and inequalities.

Achieving gender equality and realizing the human rights, dignity and capabilities of diverse groups of women is a central requirement of a just and sustainable world

Increasingly, women's full participation is recognized as central to policymaking. For example, their decisive involvement in community forest management bodies yields positive outcomes for both forest sustainability and gender equality (Agarwal, 2010). Further, certain aspects of gender equality, such as female education and women's share of employment, can have a positive impact on economic growth, although this impact is dependent on the nature of growth strategies, the structure of the economy, the sectoral composition of women's employment and labour market segregation, among other factors (Kabeer and Natali, 2013).

However, while gender equality can have a catalytic effect on achieving economic, social and environmental sustainability, the reverse does not always hold true. Hence, a simple "win-win" relationship between gender equality and sustainability cannot be assumed. Indeed, some patterns of economic growth are

Policy responses that view women as "sustainability saviours" draw upon and reinforce stereotypes regarding women's roles in relation to the family, the community and the environment. Such responses often add to women's already heavy unpaid work burdens without conferring rights, resources and benefits. Power imbalances in gender relations determine whether women's actions and work translate into the realization of their rights and capabilities. While the participation of women is vital, their involvement in policy interventions aimed at sustainability does not automatically mean greater gender equality, particularly when the structural foundations of gender inequality remain unchanged.

There are, however, alternative approaches that move towards sustainability and gender equality synergistically. Some are rooted in the everyday practices through which women and men access, control, use and manage natural resources in ways that sustain livelihoods and well-being. Joint initiatives between the State and the community in the Amazon Basin, for example, have the potential to conserve forest biodiversity and address climate change mitigation while providing for local sustainable livelihoods of women and men (Rival, 2012). Others are evident in movements and collectivities, many of them led by women, to build food and resource sovereignty and sustainable communities and cities. For example, in South Asia, a network of grass-roots women leaders are working to scale up capacity to reduce risks and vulnerabilities to climate change in their communities and build a culture of resilience.[3]

B/ MESSAGES OF THIS WORLD SURVEY

The aims of the present *World Survey* are to chart why and how gender equality must be at the centre of sustainable development and the actions necessary to achieve sustainable development with gender equality. The overall messages of the report are:

(a) Forging any sustainable development pathway must include an explicit commitment to gender equality, women's empowerment and women's rights in its conceptualization and implementation;

(b) Achieving sustainable development means recognizing the synergies between gender equality and sustainability and engaging with the tensions and trade-offs that inevitably arise between the three dimensions of sustainability and with the integration of gender equality;

(c) Addressing the trade-offs and negotiating the policy dilemmas to achieve sustainable development and gender equality requires inclusive deliberation processes and ways to monitor exclusions and trade-offs. The active participation, leadership and creativity of civil society and women's organizations, communities and concerned individuals are critical to such deliberations.

The *World Survey* does not attempt to cover the exceedingly wide range of important and necessary aspects of sustainable development with gender equality. Rather, it delves into a selected set of topics that are fundamental to women's lives, strategic for achieving gender equality and closely intertwined with the economic, social and environmental dimensions of sustainability: patterns of growth, employment generation and "public goods"[4] provisioning; food production, distribution and consumption; population and women's bodily integrity; and water, sanitation and energy. The chapters thus discuss different tangible elements of sustainable livelihoods for women within the overarching frame of gender-responsive economic, social and environmental sustainability.

Chapter 2 articulates what sustainable development with gender equality means for policymaking purposes: economic, social and environmental development that ensures human well-being and dignity, ecological integrity, gender equality and social justice, now and in the future. Recognizing that governments will need to assess complex policy options, in which there will inevitably be tensions and trade-offs, the *World Survey* proposes criteria for policymakers, in order to enable them to evaluate policies for sustainable development and gender equality.

Each chapter thereafter shows how unsustainable development patterns and gender inequality reinforce each other. Chapter 3, on the green economy, gender equality and care, elaborates on the interactions between growth trajectories and rising inequalities, underscoring the exploitation of women's labour through low wages and reliance on extensive and unpaid care work.

Chapter 4, on food security and gender equality, illustrates how systemic dynamics in the global economy and markets are intersecting with gender relations to have deleterious consequences for both household food security and gender equality. Yet dominant perspectives, in this case the productionist focus that has dominated much international thinking and policy since the 1980s, marginalize the question of the right to food. The chapter shows how the volatility of world cereal markets, low wages and precarious livelihoods interact with gender-specific constraints around resource rights, access and control. The effects of climate change and of large-scale land investments for export crops and biofuels are adding to such constraints. Women farmers are central in producing food for their families and in sustaining the ecologies that enable this, but must often do so under increasingly constrained conditions.

Chapter 5, on population, sustainable development and gender equality, shows the continued and indeed, renewed, dominance of policy perspectives that attribute environmental degradation and ecological threats to growing populations. These perspectives distract attention from and thus support the continuation of unsustainable consumption and production patterns and inequities that are actually far more significant in producing environmental problems than are sheer numbers of people. The chapter discusses the dangers of narrowly focused population policies that view women's fertility as a cause of and solution for environmental degradation and that can be coercive and punitive, without providing support for — and in fact, often undermining — women's rights, dignity and control over their bodies.

Each chapter also shows that alternative pathways that move in sustainable directions, economically, socially and environmentally, are possible. They are underpinned by alternative visions and values that emphasize not just profit and growth, but the importance of sustainability, gender equality, inclusivity and social justice. Typically, they involve different combinations of public, private and civil society institutions and require strong state action. States play central roles as duty bearers in delivering on commitments to gender equality, providing appropriate policy contexts, setting standards and regulating resource use, holding private actors to account and, crucially, providing public services and investments for social and ecological sustainability. Social movements are key in initiating and demanding such alternatives and in shaping forms of collective action that maintain them.

Thus, in relation to paid work and public goods (see chap. 3), new public and private alliances pushing for and building green economies and green transformations are highlighted. Here, pathways are emerging that link financing, technologies and investments in areas such as low-carbon and renewable energy towards modes of growth that respect ecological limits. Building on existing practices and policy proposals, the chapter underscores the economic, social and environmental pay-offs and benefits for gender equality of improved earnings and employment conditions for workers providing such environmental services as waste-picking and recycling, and also for those providing care-related personal services. In relation to food (see chap. 4), the *World Survey* emphasizes a strong focus on securing the right to food. This includes policy and public support for smallholder farming, particularly for women smallholders, enabling them to secure ecologically-sound cultivation, maintain soil fertility and ensure their livelihoods. Successful examples often incorporate local knowledge of ecological conditions, soils and seeds; cooperatives for production and marketing; and support, such as credit to enable poorer farmers to access appropriate inputs. State interventions, for instance in setting minimum wages and price regulation, and international negotiations around such issues as export subsidies and the maintenance of reserve stocks to offset price volatility, also support access and rights to food.

The chapter on investments for gender-responsive sustainable development (see chap. 6) highlights the ways in which the poorest women and girls can secure rights to products and services that meet essential everyday needs for water, sanitation, clean cooking and electricity. These investments bring essential benefits both in terms of environmental sustainability and in enhancing people's capabilities, dignity and health. Public investment is key to such initiatives, but so too is innovation to find appropriate technologies and attune them to local social and ecological conditions. The role of local knowledge and grass-roots innovation and action therefore prove to be critical in this context too. The challenge is then to scale up equitably while maintaining a focus on gender equality and sustainability.

Each chapter emphasizes that women's agency is central to many of these sustainable development pathways. They are often at the forefront of social movements, resisting unsustainable models and demanding alternatives. Their knowledge, innovation, action and agency is central to finding, demonstrating and building more economically, socially and ecologically sustainable ways to manage local ecologies, adapt to climate change, produce and access food and secure sustainable and appropriate water, sanitation and energy services. For pathways to be truly sustainable and advance gender equality and the rights and capabilities of women and girls, those whose lives and well-being are at stake must be involved in decision-making and leading the way, through community groups, women's organizations and other forms of collective action and engagement.

The *World Survey* concludes with recommendations for concrete policy actions to move towards sustainable development and gender equality. Given the diversity of contexts within which policymakers operate, rather than being prescriptive, the *World Survey* identifies three criteria for assessing if policies, programmes and actions taken in the name of sustainability are likely to achieve gender equality and women's rights, especially the rights of marginalized groups, who are likely to bear a disproportionate share of the costs of economic, social and environmental unsustainability. The overall message of the *World Survey* is one of optimism and hope, that the world can forge a more economically, socially and environmentally sustainable future, in which women and girls, men and boys can enjoy their human rights to the full.

For pathways to be truly sustainable and advance gender equality, those whose lives and well-being are at stake
must be involved in decision-making and leading the way, through collective action and engagement

CHAPTER /2
GENDER EQUALITY AND SUSTAINABLE DEVELOPMENT

A/ INTRODUCTION

The imperatives of achieving gender equality and attaining sustainable development were clearly acknowledged in the outcome document of the United Nations Conference on Sustainable Development:

We recognize that gender equality and women's empowerment are important for sustainable development and our common future. We reaffirm our commitments to ensure women's equal rights, access and opportunities for participation and leadership in the economy, society and political decision-making. ... We underscore that women have a vital role to play in achieving sustainable development. We recognize the leadership role of women, and we resolve to promote gender equality and women's empowerment and to ensure their full and effective participation in sustainable development policies, programmes and decision-making at all levels.
(General Assembly resolution 66/288, annex, paras. 31 and 45).

The *World Survey* articulates what sustainable development with gender equality could mean for policies, programmes and decision-making at all levels in the current global juncture. In doing so it reflects on the early twenty-first century global context, when entrenched poverty and hunger, rising inequalities, ecosystem destruction and climate change, all of which

are consequences, in large part, of prevailing economic models and paradigms, pose unprecedented challenges for the realization of women's rights and risk undermining further the sustainability of their households, communities and societies. Dominant development patterns have both entrenched gender inequalities and proved unsustainable as regards many issues covered in the *World Survey,* including economic growth and work; population and reproduction; food and agriculture; and water, sanitation and energy. Yet the overall message of the *World Survey* is one of hope in the possibilities of constructing, through vigorous democratic deliberation that involves states, women and men, civil society organizations, the private sector and global institutions, alternative development trajectories within which gender equality and sustainability can powerfully reinforce each other.

International norms and standards on women's and girls' human rights and gender equality provide a solid basis for advancing action to strengthen the vital role of women in achieving sustainable development. Discrimination on the basis of sex is prohibited under all major international human rights instruments. The Convention on the Elimination of All Forms of Discrimination against Women[5] obligates States parties to take all appropriate measures to ensure the full development and advancement

International norms and standards on women's and girls' human rights and gender equality provide a solid basis for advancing action to strengthen the vital role of women in achieving sustainable development of women. International Labour Organization (ILO) conventions have continuously enhanced women's rights to and at work, including, most recently, those of domestic workers.

The series of United Nations conferences convened during the 1990s advanced international norms and agreements on sustainable development and gender equality, the empowerment of women and the human rights of women and girls.

The United Nations Conference on Environment and Development, held in 1992, provided a landmark forum to advance the global policy framework on sustainable development. It launched Agenda 21, a commitment to sustainable development and three global environmental conventions — the United Nations Framework Convention on Climate Change,[6] the Convention on Biological Diversity[7] and the United Nations Convention to Combat Desertification in Those Countries Experiencing Serious Drought and/or Desertification, Particularly in Africa.[8] Principle 20 of the Rio Declaration on Environment and Development[1] states that the full participation of women is essential to achieving sustainable development. The Convention on Biological Diversity recognizes that the integration of women's rights and gender equality in biodiversity conservation and sustainable use is not only intrinsically important, but can also improve the efficacy of interventions, programmes and resources.

In 1993, the World Conference on Human Rights, held in Vienna, affirmed, in the Vienna Declaration and Programme of Action, that the "human rights of women and of the girl-child are an inalienable, integral and indivisible part of universal human rights" (A/CONF.157/24 (Part I), chap. III).

The Programme of Action of the International Conference on Population and Development,[9] adopted in 1994, marked the beginning of a new chapter on the interrelationship between population, human rights and sustainable development. The outcome positioned gender equality and the empowerment of women as global priorities and emphasized the well-being of individuals as the key focus of the global agenda on population and sustainable development. The Programme of Action highlights a number of critical areas for advancing gender equality, including universal access to family planning and sexual and reproductive health services and reproductive rights; equal access to education for girls; and equal sharing of responsibilities for care and housework between women and men.

The Beijing Declaration and Platform for Action,[2] adopted in 1995, set a landmark global agenda for women's human rights, gender equality and the empowerment of women. The Declaration provides that "the advancement of women and the achievement of equality between women and men are a matter of human rights and a condition for social justice and ... are the only way to build a sustainable, just and developed society". The Platform for Action calls on governments to integrate gender concerns and perspectives into policies and programmes for sustainable development. The upcoming 20-year global review and appraisal of the implementation of the Beijing Platform for Action provides an important opportunity for renewed commitments for accelerated action.

The Rome Declaration on World Food Security and the World Food Summit Plan of Action[10] adopted in 1996, urged governments to "ensure an enabling political, social, and economic environment designed to create the best conditions for the eradication of poverty and for durable peace, based on full and equal participation of women and men, which is most conducive to achieving sustainable food security for all".

The United Nations Millennium Declaration, adopted in 2000, built upon the outcomes of the major summits and world conferences

The upcoming 20-year global review and appraisal of the implementation of the Beijing Platform for Action provides an important opportunity for renewed commitments for accelerated action

of the 1990s. In the Millennium Declaration, Member States affirmed six fundamental principles essential to international relations, namely freedom, equality, solidarity, tolerance, respect for nature and shared responsibility, and called for action in key areas, including development and poverty eradication, peace and security, and democracy and human rights. Governments also confirmed their resolve to promote gender equality and the empowerment of women as effective ways to combat poverty, hunger and disease and to promote sustainable development (General Assembly resolution 55/2).

More recently, the importance of women's participation in decision-making regarding climate change has been recognized at the global level. The Conference of the Parties to the United Nations Framework Convention on Climate Change, at its eighteenth session, in 2012, adopted a decision to promote the goal of gender balance in the bodies of and delegations to the sessions of the Conference of the Parties and to include gender and climate change as a standing item on the agenda of the Conference (See FCCC/CP/2012/8/ADD.3, decision 23/CP.18).

Recent resolutions adopted by the General Assembly have further reaffirmed the centrality of gender equality to sustainable development. In General Assembly resolution 68/139 on the improvement of the situation of women in rural areas, adopted at its sixty-eighth session, the Assembly urged Member States to mainstream gender considerations in the governance of natural resources and to leverage the participation and influence of women in managing the sustainable use of natural resources. The resolution also called upon governments to support women smallholder farmers by facilitating their access to extension and financial services, agricultural inputs and land, water sanitation and irrigation, markets and innovative technologies. In resolution 68/227 on women in development, adopted at the same session, the Assembly encouraged governments to take measures to ensure equal access to full and productive employment and decent work.

Similarly, the agreed conclusions of the Commission on the Status of Women have advanced the global policy framework on gender equality and sustainable development. At its fifty-eighth session, the Commission urged governments to promote the full and equal participation of women and men as agents and beneficiaries of people-centred sustainable development (see E/2014/27). The Commission also emphasized the need for governments to value, reduce and redistribute unpaid care work by prioritizing social protection policies, accessible and affordable social services and the development of infrastructure, including access to environmentally sound time- and energy-saving technologies.

B/ A TIME OF CHALLENGES AND OPPORTUNITIES

It is increasingly clear that dominant patterns of development and growth are unsustainable in economic, social and environmental terms (ILO, 2012; A/CONF.216/PC/7). They have led to increasingly precarious livelihoods, with 1.2 billion people living in extreme poverty (United Nations, 2013a) and many more without access to basic services and social protections. Current patterns of growth have coincided with rising inequalities in wealth, income and capabilities worldwide, across and between nations (United Nations, 2013b; United Nations Development Programme (UNDP), 2013a). Although some developing countries with rising incomes are catching up with developed countries, incomes in the latter are still much higher than those in the converging countries. The poorest 5 per cent of the population in a high-income developed country tends to be richer than two thirds of the population in a low-income developing country. Income still "depends on citizenship and location" (United Nations Research Institute for Social Development (UNRISD), 2012a). In this context, gender inequalities across economic, social and environmental dimensions remain widespread and persistent.

Human activities have become key drivers of earth system processes and are manifested in the depletion and degradation of natural resources; the loss of key ecosystems, habitats and biodiversity; the pollution of land, oceans and the atmosphere; and in climate change, with concomitant severe and unpredictable weather effects as humanity approaches or exceeds what have been referred to as "planetary boundaries" (Intergovernmental Panel on Climate Change, 2013; Rockström and others, 2009). In recent years such processes have produced unprecedented shocks and stresses, reflected in floods, droughts, devastated urban and rural landscapes and livelihoods, with many people and places suffering from a confluence of food, climate and financial crises. These crises of unsustainability potentially affect all and carry profound risks for future generations, as described in 1987 in the Report of the World Commission on Environment and Development, "Our common future" (A/42/427, annex).

1. Patterns of unsustainable development and gender inequality

The underlying causes and consequences of unsustainability and gender inequality are deeply intertwined and rooted in the dominant economic models (Fukuda-Parr, Heintz and Seguino, 2013). These involve economic liberalization and the concentration of productive and financial activity geared to short-term profits; unrestrained material consumption; unparalleled levels of militarism; and the privatization of public goods and services, all at the expense of state regulation and redistribution. Such processes have caused, in many places, crises of care, which means the breakdown in the abilities of individuals, families, communities and societies to sustain, care for and educate themselves and future generations, thereby undermining people's rights and dignity (United Nations Entity for Gender Equality and the Empowerment of Women (UN-Women), 2014).

Financial crises and recessions, which have taken hold in many countries with severe repercussions across the world, have brought to the fore the risks and vulnerabilities inherent to liberalized and financialized market models. These risks and vulnerabilities undermine the viability of market models even on their own terms. The fruits of economic growth have also been unequally divided. Over the past three decades, economic disparities between and within countries and regions have increased.

The richest 1 per cent of the world's population owns some 40 per cent of all assets while the poorer half of the population owns just 1 per cent of global assets (UNDP, 2013a). The world's most rapidly growing economies, including those of Asia, Southern Africa and Latin America, have also seen rapid rises in inequality. Inequality itself threatens economic sustainability, fuelling unrest and conflict and undermining the stability, level playing field and consumer demand on which growth relies (Stiglitz, 2012).

The dominant economic models are unsustainable, not only in economic terms but also in social and environmental terms, perpetuating gender and other inequalities and damaging ecosystems and biodiversity (ILO, 2012; A/CONF.216/PC/7). Export-oriented models of growth in many areas of industry and agriculture have contributed to the rising labour force participation of women, as discussed in the 1999 *World Survey* (A/54/227).[11] Yet gender-based discrimination and segregation in labour markets, as well as the weak regulation of those markets, have served to confine women to jobs that are low-paid and of poor quality in terms of working conditions and access to social protection. They reinforce the status of women as secondary earners within their households (Chen and others, 2005).

Moreover, markets can continue to function as they do because of their reliance on the unpaid work that is allocated to caring for children, the sick and the elderly and the domestic work that sustains households and communities (UNRISD, 2010). Economic growth could not take place without this unpaid and often invisible work. Dominant growth models also rely on the exploitation of natural resources as if these were unlimited. The environmental costs of production, such as pollution, toxic waste and greenhouse gas emissions are externalized. That is, "climate change, like other environmental

problems, involves an externality: the emission of greenhouse gases damages others at no cost to the agent responsible for the emissions" (Stern, 2006). Such patterns of development create profits at environmental expense, whether through the entrenched fossil fuel systems that supply industry, energy and automobiles, or through industrial agriculture that generates short-term gain by mining soils and depleting water resources. Such patterns are unsustainable, compromising future production and consumption and threatening the integrity and resilience of ecosystems and biodiversity (Millennium Ecosystem Assessment, 2005).

Declines in ecosystem services and productive capacity destabilize people's livelihoods and health, both in the present and for future generations. In the pursuit of profit, the social and environmental costs of production are shifted onto the state, private households and local communities, or onto the natural environment. The costs and consequences of socio-environmental change are manifested in different forms of gender inequality. Natural disasters, including those related to climate change, disproportionately affect poor women (Neumayer and Plümper, 2007). Women often bear the brunt of coping with climate-related shocks and stresses or the health effects of indoor and urban pollution, which add to their care burdens. As land, forest and water resources once held in common are increasingly enclosed, privatized or "grabbed" for commercial investment, local communities and indigenous peoples, particularly women, whose livelihoods depend on them, are marginalized and displaced (White and White, 2012; Levien, 2012; FAO, 2012). In this process, sustainable livelihoods, health, rights and dignity are jeopardized (Unmüßig, 2014).

2. Responding to the challenges

Growing international attention and debate has recognized the clear need to move economies and societies onto more sustainable paths, whether to avert crisis and catastrophe, or enable prosperity through green economies. In an attempt to regulate greenhouse gas emissions, carbon emissions have been monetized and

Economic growth cannot take place without unpaid work

traded on world markets. Biodiversity offset schemes posit that the destruction of biodiversity can be compensated by creating similar habitats elsewhere. Payments for ecosystem services compensate communities and individuals for conserving and protecting such essential natural goods as water sources and forests. Such schemes aim to assign value to natural capital so it can be internalized in economic calculations. However, the resulting transactions and markets have often militated against equal access to and benefit from natural resources for women and men because of power differentials and the lack of participation in decision-making and negotiations (McAfee, 2012; UNRISD, 2012b) (see box I). They have also further intensified pressures on natural resources through land, water and green "grabs" (Unmüßig, 2014; Fairhead, Leach and Scoones, 2012; Mehta, Veldwisch and Franco, 2012).

Women's knowledge, agency and collective action are central to finding, demonstrating and building more economically, socially and environmentally sustainable pathways to manage local landscapes; adapt to climate change; produce and access food; and secure sustainable water, sanitation and energy services. For example women's decisive involvement in community forest management bodies yields positive outcomes for both forest sustainability and gender equality (Agarwal, 2010) (see box I). Thus governments and donor agencies target women as critical agents for community adaptation to climate change; in their role as smallholder farmers, the mainstay of sustainable food production; and through limiting their reproductive rights, as the answer to population-environment problems. Indeed, perspectives that view women narrowly as "sustainability saviours" are evident in many areas, from the conservation of biodiversity, water and soils to building socially and environmentally sustainable services.

Yet viewing women as sustainability saviours carries dangers. Such approaches are based on the assumption that women's time is an "infinitely elastic" (Elson, 1996) and unlimited resource that can be drawn upon to sustain people and environments, without due consideration for women's own health and well-being and the competing demands on their time. Policies that are based on stereotypical assumptions regarding women's caring role in the family, community and environment treat women as a homogeneous category. They ignore the vital intersections with other inequalities that shape women's interests, knowledge, values, opportunities and capabilities. Power imbalances in gender relations, in the exercise of rights, access to and control of resources, or participation in decision-making, determine whether women's actions and work translate into enhanced rights and capabilities, dignity and bodily integrity. Thus women's involvement in policy interventions ostensibly aimed at sustainability does not automatically mean greater gender equality; on the contrary, intensifying women's workloads to benefit the community and the environment can entrench and worsen gender inequalities.

Despite some of the shortcomings in the ways in which policy actors have responded to sustainability challenges, this is also a time of opportunity. There are many concrete examples from around the world of alternative pathways that move towards sustainability and gender equality. Some of these are emerging from women's and men's everyday practices of accessing, controlling, using and managing forests, soils, water and urban landscapes in ways that sustain their livelihoods and enhance their well-being.

Women have been and can be central actors in pathways to sustainability and green transformation. However, crucially, this must not mean adding environmental conservation to women's unpaid care work. It means recognition and respect for their knowledge, rights, capabilities and bodily integrity, and ensuring that roles are matched with rights, control over resources and decision-making power. Gender equality and sustainable development can reinforce each other in powerful ways and charting such pathways and concrete areas for policy action is a central aim of the *World Survey*.

Box I

Sustainable forest management and gender equality

Forest landscapes illustrate well the interaction between economic, social and ecological processes in shaping change. Vegetation cover and quality reflect the dynamic interaction of ecologies with people's livelihoods. The same forests and trees may be valued by different people for their timber and gathered products, for their services in shade and ecosystem protection, or for their cultural values.

Forests have been subject to policies and interventions, with varying outcomes for gender equality. From colonial times onwards, successive state, donor-led and non-governmental programmes have focused on goals ranging from sustaining supplies of timber and non-forest products to protecting watersheds and biodiversity. The latest round of interventions focuses on mitigating climate change. The objective is to manage forests in order to protect and enhance carbon stocks as a means of offsetting emissions produced in industrialized settings. The many schemes that have emerged, associated variously with the United Nations Collaborative Programme on Reducing Emissions from Deforestation and Forest Degradation in Developing Countries (REDD process), the Clean Development Mechanism, the Verified Carbon Standard or unaccredited private deals, all re-value forests as a source of a carbon commodity to be exchanged in emerging markets. As these forest carbon projects play out on the ground, they have tried to meet global sustainability needs but have often excluded local forest users and undermined their livelihoods, thereby contributing to dispossession (Corbera and Brown, 2008; Corbera and Schroeder, 2010). The result is often greater inequality and injustice for local users vis-à-vis external agencies and global actors. A recent study on REDD+* concludes that women are not "key stakeholders or beneficiaries of REDD+ because of their invisibility in the forest sector — largely viewed as a masculine domain" (Women Organizing for Change in Agriculture and Natural Resource Management and others, 2013).

Alternatives have focused on community-based and joint forest management. Such approaches have the potential to foster and support local rights and capabilities, including those of women. Yet the outcomes of community forest management for gender equality have varied considerably. In many cases, gendered interests and values in forest management have been subordinated to a generalized notion of "the community", through institutions dominated by men and community leaders. However, work in Nepal and in Gujarat, India, provides evidence to show that gender equality in joint forest management processes is associated with positive outcomes both for forest ecology and for gender equality (Agarwal, 2010). Gender-related inequality (unless mitigated by specific measures) is often associated with low or failed cooperation within forest management committees. Where women are full participants, with a voice and power in committee structures, their equal access to resources is enabled along with a more equitable sharing of benefits and improved forest sustainability.

* The United Nations Collaborative Programme on Reducing Emissions from Deforestation and Forest Degradation in Developing Countries (REDD) is an effort to create a financial value for the carbon stored in forests, offering incentives for developing countries to reduce emissions from forested lands and invest in low-carbon paths to sustainable development. REDD+ goes beyond deforestation and forest degradation, and includes the role of conservation, the sustainable management of forests and enhancement of forest carbon stocks. See www.un-redd.org (accessed 29 June 2014).

C/ SUSTAINABLE DEVELOPMENT WITH GENDER EQUALITY: DEFINITIONS AND CONCEPTS

The understanding of sustainable development for the present *World Survey* is in line with the definition proposed, in 1987, in the landmark report of the World Commission on Environment and Development: sustainable development should "meet the needs of the present without compromising the ability of future generations to meet their own needs" (A/42/427, annex), which involves integrating the three pillars of sustainability: economic, social and environmental.

Sustainable development is economic, social and environmental development that ensures human well-being and dignity, ecological integrity, gender equality and social justice, now and in the future

The *World Survey* builds on this broad definition in several important respects that contribute to the ongoing deliberations on the post-2015 development framework. It re emphasizes normative values, anchoring its policy analysis within a human rights and human capabilities framework, as elaborated below, and underlines that questions of equality and justice are important for present as well as future generations. In both aspects, gender equality is central.

Sustainable development, therefore, is economic, social and environmental development that ensures human well-being and dignity, ecological integrity, gender equality and social justice, now and in the future.

The understanding of gender equality for the purpose of the *World Survey* is that elaborated by the Committee on the Elimination of Discrimination against Women, which clarified that: "... a purely formal legal or programmatic approach is not sufficient to achieve women's de facto equality with men, which the Committee interprets as substantive equality. In addition, the Convention requires that women be given an equal start and that they be empowered by an enabling environment to achieve equality of results" (see A/59/38, part one, annex I, General Recommendation No. 25). Substantive or de facto equality therefore entails women's equal enjoyment of their rights, especially in regard to results and outcomes. To ensure this, States must not only eliminate all forms of discrimination against women, including structural and historic discrimination, by building on the foundations of formal or legal equality, but ensure the realization of their rights.

This concept of substantive gender equality resonates strongly with the capabilities framework, which draws attention to the substantive freedoms that people have "to lead the kinds of lives they value — and have reason to value" (Sen, 1999). The human rights and capabilities frameworks share a common motivation, which is the freedom and dignity of the individual, and both stand in sharp contrast to dominant economic approaches that emphasize the expansion of gross domestic product (GDP) as their principal goals (Vizard, Fukuda-Parr and Elson, 2011). Deprivation of elementary capabilities, which may be reflected in premature mortality, significant undernourishment and widespread illiteracy (Sen, 1999, p. 20), continues to mark the lives of millions of people around the world, even in countries with high rates of economic growth. Such deprivation in rights and capabilities can also be experienced by women and girls who are members of households that may not be considered poor or deprived at an aggregate level, underlining the need to always look behind averages and aggregates. While the removal of such inequalities in basic well-being is of utmost importance, the capabilities framework, like the human rights approach, also draws attention to the significance of the agency of women because of its intrinsic value and because the "limited role of women's active agency seriously afflicts the lives of all people — men as well as women, children as well as adults" (Sen 1999, 191). Both human rights and capabilities frameworks underscore the potential synergy between women's agency and well-being outcomes, and the indivisibility of their rights.

The issue of intergenerational justice, which is a key component of the definition of sustainability in the report of the World Commission on Environment and Development, remains an important concern today, especially in

a post-crisis context when the prospect of realizing the rights to decent and sustainable livelihoods for younger and future generations looks dim (United Nations, 2013b). The issue of intergenerational justice demands that the actions of the present generation do not compromise the ability of future generations to live fulfilling lives. As Anand and Sen (2000) remark "there would, however, be something distinctly odd if we were deeply concerned for the well-being of the future — and as yet unborn — generations while ignoring the plight of the poor today". This concern directs attention to inequalities now. The depth and scale of multiple inequalities that characterize the bulk of countries today, both developing and developed, demand action. Inequality harms economic dynamism and poverty reduction, can trigger economic crises, creates social exclusion and feeds into political tensions and conflicts. Redistributive measures that address inequalities and realize human rights and capabilities need to be prioritized as central to sustainable development. The participation and voice of marginalized groups in decision-making at multiple levels is also essential (UNDP, 2013a).

D/ LOOKING BACK, MOVING FORWARD: LEARNING FROM ACTION ON GENDER EQUALITY AND SUSTAINABLE DEVELOPMENT

From the early 1970s, social and environmental movements in Asian, Latin American and African settings mainly focused on the negative impacts of economic development on the livelihoods, rights and well-being of local and indigenous peoples. Examples

include movements resisting large dams and accompanying displacements, and mining and forest destruction (Doyle, 2005). The Chipko movement that resisted industrial logging in the Himalayas was primarily motivated by forest and livelihood protection. It went on to become a celebrated symbol for non-violent environmental protest and the significance of women's participation. Similar symbolism is associated with Kenya's Green Belt Movement, founded by Wangari Maathai in 1977, which encouraged rural women to collectively plant trees for sustainable livelihoods and forest conservation.

In developed countries, movements have focused on combating pollution, resource depletion and habitat loss as well as militarism and nuclear power, and on promoting peace. Together with cornerstone publications such as *Silent Spring* (Carson, 1962) and *The Limits to Growth: A Report to the Club of Rome's Project on the Predicament of Mankind* (Meadows and others, 1972), they fuelled a growing public and political consciousness of the environmental and social downsides of prevailing models.

The United Nations Conference on Environment and Development, held in Rio de Janeiro, Brazil, in 1992, provided a landmark forum where diverse approaches to sustainable development were debated by governments, civil society and social movements. The "local Agenda 21" initiative envisaged sustainability being built from the bottom up through initiatives by local governments, community groups and women and men. It stimulated a plethora of community-based and joint state-local sustainable development projects and programmes across the world, around sustainable agriculture and land use, water, fisheries, forests, wildlife, urban environments and other issues. These initiatives embodied important recognition of local resource rights and collective action. Yet many suffered from an overly homogeneous view of "the community" that failed to account for socially- and gender-differentiated perspectives and priorities (Dressler and others, 2010; Leach, Mearns and Scoones, 1999), or involved women only in a tokenistic manner in project management committees. The lack of attention to gender inequalities and other inequalities has continued, to the present day, in many

initiatives for community-based sustainable development (Harcourt, 2012).

In the run-up to the United Nations Conference on Environment and Development, a wide coalition of non-governmental organizations and social movements, including the Women's Environment and Development Organization, Development Alternatives with Women for a New Era and others, advocated to integrate gender concerns into emerging sustainable development debates. Development Alternatives with Women for a New Era, along with other groups, called for the transformation of growth-based development models towards gender-responsive development (Wiltshire, 1992). Women's Action Agenda 21, a platform of various groups, critiqued existing development pathways and free market thinking, instead embracing the concept of sustainable livelihoods and highlighting the need to link everyday practices of care with resource justice (Wichterich, 2012). Yet many of the alternatives put forward by women's groups and networks in the global women's lobby at the Conference were overshadowed by the prevailing optimism about economic efficiency, technology and markets.

Agenda 21 and debates from 1992 onwards recognized women as important actors in environmental protection and poverty alleviation, but tended to treat women in an instrumentalist way. Women were considered the primary users and effective managers and conservers of the environment at the local level (see, for example, Dankelman and Davidson, 1988; Rodda, 1991). This underpinned the view that women should be harnessed as sustainability saviours, based on the assumption that women are especially close to nature. Women-environment connections, especially in domestic and subsistence activities such as collecting fuelwood, hauling water and cultivating food, were often presented as if they were natural and universal, rather than as the product of particular social and cultural norms and expectations. Ensuing projects and policies often mobilized and instrumentalized women's labour, skills and knowledge, thereby adding to

Policies should ensure women's effective participation in and equal benefit from sustainable development projects and actively address entrenched discriminatory stereotypes and inequalities

their unpaid work without addressing whether they had the rights, voice and power to control project benefits.

A number of useful lessons emerge from this history for policymaking. First, policymakers should avoid making broad and stereotypical assumptions about women's and men's relationships with the environment. Rather, policies should respond to the specific social context and gender power relations. For instance, women's close involvement in gathering wild foods and other forest products might reflect labour and land tenure relations and their lack of access to income with which to purchase food, rather than reflecting their closeness to nature (Rocheleau, 1988; Agarwal, 1992). Second, policies should be responsive to differences in how diverse groups of women and men engage with land, trees, water and other resources. Third, policies should pay special attention to women's rights in regard to tenure and property, as well as control over labour, resources, products and decisions within both the household and the community. Finally, policies should ensure women's effective participation in and equal benefit from sustainable development projects and actively address entrenched discriminatory stereotypes and inequalities.

United Nations Conference on Sustainable Development: three important policy debates

In the run-up to the United Nations Conference on Sustainable Development, held in 2012, the potential pathways to sustainable development were the subject of deliberation in the context of climate, food and finance crises. In that context, many policy and business actors embraced positive alignments between economic growth and environmental concerns through such notions as the green economy, in the name of sustainable development. Social movements, on the other hand, proposed alternative perspectives on issues such as climate change, water privatization, genetically modified organisms, biodiversity and "land grabbing", and advocated pathways that link sustainable development firmly with questions of social justice. In this context, debates have continued between key actors on the topics of climate change, planetary boundaries and the green economy, which are elaborated upon below, with a focus on their gender dimensions.

Since the 1990s, climate change has become one of the defining challenges of the modern world. The relative successes and setbacks of global climate change frameworks and negotiations, difficulties in implementing the principle of common but differentiated responsibilities in mitigating far-reaching threats, and the plight and coping strategies of people who must adapt to climate-related shocks and stresses have galvanized public reaction.[12] This has taken the form of renewed and globalized social and environmental movements and campaigns, stretching across local and global scales. The United Nations Framework Convention on Climate Change was weak on gender equality, and despite the sustained engagement and efforts of gender equality advocates, subsequent efforts to mainstream gender issues into climate change debates have been piecemeal (UN-Women and Mary Robinson Foundation — Climate Justice, 2013).

Responses to climate change that address gender issues tend to view women as victims of climate impacts, or entrench stereotypes and roles of women as natural carers keeping their communities resilient or adopting low-carbon options. Yet gender and class relations, rights and inequalities shape differences in women's and men's vulnerabilities to climate change and their opportunities to be agents in mitigation and adaptation (Agarwal, 2002). In contexts of entrenched discrimination, where women's active participation and decision-making power is constrained, women's formal inclusion in technical committees for low-carbon technologies can be a first step, but women's participation can only be effective and meaningful when underlying gender power relations are transformed and when attention and support are given to women's specific knowledge and capacities (Wong, 2009; Otzelberger, 2011).

Much of the debate on gender and climate change has focused on adaptation and local-level vulnerabilities. Only recently, more limited attention has been given to gender perspectives in discussions involving large-scale technology, market initiatives and climate finance (Schalatek, 2013; World Bank, 2011). Commitments to achieve gender equality, such as those contained in the Convention on the Elimination of All Forms of Discrimination against Women, are insufficiently reflected in national adaptation or low-carbon development plans (Otzelberger, 2011). This poor integration is a reflection of and in turn, reinforces, the tendency for policy to focus on simplistic solutions, rather than the more structural political and economic changes needed to redirect pathways of climate unsustainability and gender inequality.

A second contemporary debate centres on notions of planetary boundaries. A series of nine planetary boundaries has been identified, referring to the biophysical processes in the Earth's system on which human life depends (Rockström and others, 2009). These boundaries, together, serve to keep the planet within a so-called "safe operating space" for humanity. Influential scientific analyses suggest that the world has entered the Anthropocene, a new epoch in which human activities have become the dominant driver of many earth system processes including the climate, biogeochemical cycles, ecosystems and biodiversity. Potentially catastrophic thresholds are in prospect, it is argued, providing a new urgency and authority to arguments that growth and development pathways must reconnect with the biosphere's capacity to sustain them (Folke and others, 2011).

While the science is still developing, the concept of planetary boundaries has become influential within policy debates. But the concept is also critiqued, with some actors interpreting it as anti-growth and development, while others suggest that "planetary boundaries" thinking privileges universal global environmental concerns over diverse local ones, justifying top-down interventions that protect the environment at the expense of people and their livelihoods. The renewed visions of impending scarcity and catastrophe implied by some interpretations of planetary boundaries could justify policies that limit people's rights and freedoms, as the present *World Survey* shows in relation to population. Steering development within planetary boundaries should not compromise inclusive development that respects human rights, as proposed by Raworth (2012)

Women's participation can only be effective and meaningful when underlying gender power relations are transformed and when attention and support are given to women's specific knowledge and capacities whose "doughnut" concept takes the circle of planetary boundaries and adds an inner "social foundation". In between these is a "safe and just operating space" for humanity, within which sustainable development pathways should steer (International Social Science Council, and United Nations Educational, Scientific and Cultural Organization (UNESCO), 2013). Raworth notably introduces gender equality as one dimension of this social foundation, but other discussion and advocacy arising from the planetary boundaries concept has largely been gender-blind.

Mainstream approaches to defining and developing green economies have paid little attention to their differentiated implications for women and men

Finally, green economies are now being vigorously discussed by governments, businesses and non-governmental organizations alike. According to the United Nations Environment Programme (UNEP), which launched its Green Economy Initiative in 2008, a green economy is one that results in improved human well-being and social equity, while significantly reducing environmental risks and ecological scarcities; it is low-carbon, resource-efficient and socially inclusive (UNEP, 2011). This general definition integrates economic, social and environmental concerns in ways akin to sustainable development. Yet in practice, as the *World Survey* shows, there are many versions of green economy thinking. Dominant versions assume continued, even enhanced, market-led economic growth, through green business investments and

innovations that enhance energy and resource efficiency and prevent the loss of ecosystem services. It is argued that the emerging green technology economy will be worth $4.2 trillion annually by 2020.[13] Other strands emphasize market-based approaches to environmental protection through financial valuation of natural capital, payments for ecosystem services and schemes for trading carbon and biodiversity credits and offsets.

Others argue that environmental constraints require rethinking growth and market strategies. The concept of decoupling proposed by UNEP and others (Fischer-Kowalski and others, 2011) suggests that economic growth should be delinked from the increasing consumption of material resources such as construction minerals, fossil fuels and biomass. Jackson (2011) argues for a shift in focus towards prosperity and well-being with reduced or no growth, in which investments in services and care, as well as in green action in the areas of sustainable food production and clean energy, are key.

Mainstream approaches to defining and developing green economies have paid little attention to their differentiated implications for women and men (Guerrero and Stock, 2012; Cela, Dankelman and Stern, 2013). Many gender analysts and activists criticize the United Nations Conference on Sustainable Development for having missed a chance to break with the business-as-usual global economic model, which produces environmental destruction, social exploitation and inequalities (Schalatek, 2013; Wichterich, 2012; Unmüßig, Sachs and Fatheuer, 2012). They see the green economy as a market-based approach that justifies the commodification of resources and commons, which undermines livelihoods and dispossesses local peoples, especially women food producers. Gender equality advocates call instead for green development that respects commons and livelihoods (Agarwal, 2012); and for recognition and value of care in green economy debates (Vaughan, 2007; Mellor, 2009).

E/ TOWARDS SUSTAINABLE DEVELOPMENT AND GENDER EQUALITY: IMPLICATIONS FOR POLICY ACTION

The attainment of sustainable development and gender equality potentially involves trade-offs that need to be openly discussed among different social groups (UNDP, 2011). In such negotiations, the social dimensions of sustainability — too often neglected — must be fully integrated, and states and other powerful actors must be held accountable for delivering sustainable development.

1. Bringing social sustainability to the fore

Achieving sustainable development means not only reconciling economic and environmental sustainability, but also prioritizing social sustainability. The realization of women's human rights, capabilities and well-being now and in the future requires paying specific attention to the care economy, that is, the provision of care through the family and/or household, markets, the non-profit sector and the public sector and/or state, especially the "private" domain of non-market or unpaid care work. How societies organize this work is central to their social sustainability. Policymakers rarely consider the production of human resources in the economy, apart from formal education, which is recognized for its contribution to human capital, and yet economic growth cannot take place without this unpaid and often invisible work (Folbre, 1994; UNRISD, 2010). In all societies, women typically spend more time on these non-market activities than men do, especially in contexts of environmental stress and poor infrastructure. Thus the gender division of labour between paid work and unpaid work represents a significant structural source of gender inequality.

The fact that the bulk of unpaid care work is carried out by women and girls has significant implications for their capacity to realize their rights to education, paid work, a decent standard of living and political participation (see the report of the Special Rapporteur on extreme poverty and human rights, A/68/293). In this and other domains, gender and other inequalities intersect, and it is women and girls from marginalized social groups whose capabilities and rights are most often compromised and in need of realization. Poverty and exclusion increase the amount and intensity of unpaid care work, as a result of limited access to public services and inadequate infrastructure and the lack of resources to pay for care services and time-saving technology. Unpaid care work is also intensified in contexts of economic crisis, health crises, environmental degradation, natural disasters and inadequate infrastructure and services. A just and sustainable society is one that recognizes unpaid care work by making it visible through statistics and by ensuring that policies are in place to reduce its drudgery, through appropriate public investments in infrastructure and social services, and to redistribute it between women and men within households, and between households and society more broadly.

2. Tensions and trade-offs

It is important to recognize that there may be tensions and trade-offs between the different dimensions of sustainability and with substantive gender equality, regarding the areas into which sustainability should be integrated and considerations as regards the beneficiaries of sustainable approaches (UNDP, 2011). For example, current models of economic growth increase GDP but have also led to deepening inequalities based on multiple factors. While such economic models may well perpetuate themselves over time and across regions, undeniably increasing GDP, the fact that they leave significant environmental and human costs in their wake means that they are not sustainable and thus stymie efforts to meet commitments to sustainable development.

In the pursuit of sustainability, the question of what is sustained and who benefits is central. Yet the challenges are often seen in technical and managerial terms, as a matter of getting the technologies, prices and regulations right, rather than in terms of the more profound restructuring of social, economic and political systems and power imbalances that would be required to transform unsustainable patterns. How the challenges are addressed has profound implications for who gains and who loses, among social groups and local, national and global interests.

There are many policy dilemmas to reconcile in order to ensure that women's rights and gender equality concerns are taken into account in sustainable development policies.

(OECD), for example, that entail higher prices for consumers, can have a regressive impact on poorer households, particularly given that they spend a higher proportion of their overall income on electricity (Gough, 2011). Market-based instruments that attempt to redress or prevent environmental degradation and mitigate climate change by valuing and putting a price on nature can risk exacerbating the very problems they were designed to solve. In order to reduce such risks, global and national governance and regulatory policy frameworks are necessary, as is appropriate attention to local knowledge and practices of women and men (Unmüßig, 2014; Fairhead, Leach and Scoones, 2012).

As such, women's rights advocates call for approaches that respect the commons and local livelihoods, recognize and value care, restructure production and consumption and pave the way for green transformations (Agarwal, 2010; Wichterich, 2012; Women's Major Group, 2013). Recent research on consumption patterns in Europe shows that women on average generate fewer greenhouse gas emissions than men, as a result of their greater reliance on public transport, lower consumption of meat and higher levels of energy poverty, some of which may be related

Women's rights advocates call for approaches that respect the commons and local livelihoods, recognize and value care, restructure production and consumption and pave the way for green transformations

For example, the strict conservation of carbon sinks to mitigate global climate change could undermine the local livelihood needs of women and men living near forests and intensify women's unpaid care work. Biofuel production policies could run counter to local food security needs. Carbon mitigation policies in countries which are members of the Organization for Economic Cooperation and Development

to women's lower incomes (European Institute for Gender Equality, 2012). But the same study also shows women's greater responsiveness to environmental, health and climate concerns, compared with men. These findings may very well apply globally and would have implications, for example, in terms of better provisioning of sustainable and accessible public transport and universal access to modern energy services.

Reconciling the policy dilemmas in order to achieve sustainable development with gender equality requires robust democratic spaces for deliberation, grass-roots voices and accountability mechanisms at multiple levels. Women's voices and participation in diverse forums is of critical importance, both as an issue of justice and equality and because the active presence of women can put gender-specific concerns on the agenda and contribute to collective actions that are more effective in meeting the three dimensions of sustainability (Agarwal, 2010). Enabling women's meaningful participation, however, should not mean that women carry the sole responsibility for prioritizing gender equality concerns in sustainable development policies. All decision-makers, women and men, must take responsibility.

Moving towards sustainable development and gender equality will require action at many levels by a diversity of actors and can only be achieved through democratic alliances between the state, policymakers, donors, the private and civil sectors and women and men. For such alliances to be viable, the reach and organizing power of the state are necessary. Sustainable development pathways can be conceived, inspired and piloted by non-governmental organizations, donors and private enterprises, but only the state can take them to scale, offer universal access which reaches the populations of the poor and marginalized, and provide the regulatory and institutional power to ensure sustainability. However, to ensure that the state actually delivers, civil society and social movements must have the space and mechanisms to hold decision-makers to account, which calls for renewed social contracts between the state and its people, where states fulfil their obligations, as the duty bearer, and rights holders claim and enjoy their human rights.

An enabling global context is indispensable for such social contracts to hold. The extent of global economic integration over the past decades has increased the influence and impact of a number of actors (e.g., multinational corporations or international financial institutions) on the enjoyment of human rights in many countries. These actors have an influence on the protection of labour standards, the development of infrastructure, the accessibility of public services, the protection of natural resources and access to information — all of which have serious implications for women's and girl's human rights. Hence, global governance must ensure that the actions of those actors are aligned with the efforts of governments to facilitate the realization of rights, the enhancement of capabilities and initiatives to achieve sustainable development.

States need to use their capacity and ability to deliver in ways that respect sustainability and gender equality, rather than relying on market forces. This requires accountability frameworks that secure human rights, gender equality and non-discrimination in areas like work and employment, reproduction and health, food and land and natural resource tenure. Governments also have central roles to play in providing public goods and services, supporting health, education and care for children, the elderly and the sick, which are so essential to people's capabilities, and for assuring the social dimensions of sustainability and care work. Public investment is also necessary for nurturing and scaling up key innovations for gender-responsive public goods, such as the provision of modern energy services, water supplies and appropriate sanitation facilities.

There are growing opportunities for businesses and the private sector to contribute to sustainable development solutions, as emerging green economy prospects emphasize. Nevertheless these often require state support to be viable, at least in the early stages. Meanwhile, growing evidence shows that partnership and co-production arrangements, in which private, public and civil society actors work jointly to deliver health, housing or energy services, or to manage forests, biodiversity or water, are often most effective. In order for such co-produced arrangements to work effectively for gender equality and sustainability, it is vital that women are centrally involved in planning and implementation and as such, policies must enable women's participation. Adequate financial resources are also required for achieving the goals of sustainable development (Schalatek, 2013). Approaches to participatory and gender-responsive budgeting offer prospects for gender-responsive decisions in funding allocation decisions and for ensuring accountability for tracking and reporting on gender-specific financing benchmarks.

National policies are increasingly shaped by international regimes and frameworks, globalization processes and transnational policy transfer and learning. International human rights frameworks offer important standards for holding states accountable. However, to achieve sustainable development with gender equality at its centre, women's rights need to be brought far more fully into policy frameworks. Global efforts to integrate gender equality and sustainable development thus far have been mixed, ranging from "exclusion to nominal inclusion" (Cela, Dankelman and Stern, 2013). Far more inclusion of gender equality concerns and women's participation is needed in ongoing international policy processes, through alliance-building between women's rights advocates and responsive states, as well as alliances between women's movements and other movements working on issues of social justice, equality and sustainability.

Growing evidence and analysis shows that sustainable development requires governance and action that extends from the global scale to national and local scales. This suggests a need for questions concerning gender equality and for representation of women's interests to be included by institutions from the local to the global level. Action and pressure from social movements are central in challenging and reworking the discriminatory cultures, practices, biases and stereotypes that are often evident in policy institutions and organizations.

Indeed, the growth of movements around gender equality and sustainable development is one of the most promising developments of recent years. In many countries and regions, informal economy workers, producers and consumers are organizing collectively, both to contest dominant development models and to advocate for and indeed, demonstrate, alternatives. Examples are multiplying rapidly. They include La Via Campesina, which since the 1990s has grown into a globally-networked movement to defend the rights of smallholder farmers in the face of pressures from large-scale corporate agriculture. Promoting a vision of small-scale farming rooted in agroecological techniques, local markets and food sovereignty (Borras, 2004; McMichael, 2009), some strands, though by no means all, emphasize the rights of women as small-scale food producers. The National Association of Rural and Indigenous Women in Chile, with its 10,000 members, is linked to La Via Campesina and is launching an agroecology institute to train women smallholder farmers in South America.[14] Other examples include movements initiated by groups of poor urban dwellers in many cities in Asia, Africa and Latin America, linking well-being and rights to homes and livelihoods with the design of decent, sustainable urban spaces (Satterthwaite, Mitlin and Patel, 2011). In the case of Shack/Slum Dwellers International, groups initiated around women's savings and credit associations and waste-pickers cooperatives have networked into a federated global structure that now covers 33 countries, linking local action with campaigning around global agendas. Many other examples are emerging around alternative and solidarity economies, food and land, water and energy.

In such examples, collective action, organization and cooperation provide the basis for alternative trajectories towards economic, social and environmental sustainability. Networking and alliance-building provides routes through which the everyday actions and knowledge of women and men around work, industry, land, food, water, energy and climate in diverse places can begin to scale up with appropriate state support.

Given the diversity of contexts within which policymakers operate, rather than being prescriptive, the *World Survey* identifies three criteria for assessing whether policies, programmes and actions implemented in the name of sustainability are likely to achieve gender equality and women's rights, especially the rights of marginalized groups who are likely to bear a disproportionate share of the costs of economic, social and environmental unsustainability.

The first criterion is with respect to women's capabilities and their enjoyment of human rights, particularly the capabilities and rights of the poorest and most marginalized groups. As a core criterion, policies, programmes and investments in the name of sustainable development should be assessed against compliance with human rights standards and their ability to enhance the capabilities of women and girls. No development pathway can be considered sustainable if it reduces women's capabilities and denies their human rights. In the case of population policies, for example, family planning methods that constrain women's reproductive choices and/or expose them to health risks through inappropriate contraceptive methods cannot meet the minimal criteria of sustainability proposed here.

If policies and programmes that are intended to enhance environmental sustainability inadvertently increase women's unpaid care work, then they are not on a sustainable development pathway

The second criterion is with respect to the impact on the unpaid care work of women and girls, especially from poorer and marginalized households and communities. If policies and programmes that are intended to enhance environmental sustainability inadvertently increase women's unpaid care work, then they are not on a sustainable development pathway. While there is a clear and urgent need for decarbonizing the global economy, this should include attention to local livelihoods and gender equality. For example, strict regulation of forest use that undermines local

In Krang Lahiong village (Cambodia) where she is deputy chief, Meas Sophea, a rice farmer, assists women in the community with their finances

livelihoods and intensifies women's unpaid care work is unsustainable. Conversely, investments in locally adapted and ecological technology that facilitates women's access to water sources by ensuring their affordability and quality while minimizing the distance between water sources and dwellings are clearly desirable.

The third criterion relates to the full, equal and meaningful participation of women in sustainable development, as actors, leaders and decision-makers in the processes that shape their lives as well as the future of their households, communities, nations and the world. In the area of food security, for instance, policy efforts aimed at national and local food sufficiency and low-chemical and environmentally sustainable agriculture, which are desirable objectives from the perspective of ecological sustainability, need to consult smallholder farmers, particularly women, about their priorities and constraints rather than assume that their interests are already aligned with preconceived policy aims and visions.

CHAPTER /3

GREEN ECONOMY, GENDER EQUALITY AND CARE

A/ INTRODUCTION

Growth trajectories should be assessed for their capacity to generate sustainable development. In order to ensure sustainable development with gender equality at its centre, any development policy framework needs to address a number of goals in addition to promoting growth: to reduce gender inequality, but also inequality on the basis of other factors; to create decent work and sustainable livelihoods for all; to internalize the costs of environmental degradation and climate change; and to ensure human well-being by providing public goods and supporting the care economy.

This chapter will therefore address the issue of growth and gender equality, incorporating the three dimensions of sustainable development within its analysis. It evaluates whether the dominant global economic paradigm has delivered growth and development in ways that generate sustainable livelihoods and decent work for women, considers alternative models of green economy and their implications for gender equality, as well as the implications of the current development model for people's capacity to care for each other, both within and across generations. In doing so, the chapter goes beyond the potential for "greening" jobs, to recognize that, in the light of the economic crisis of 2007-2008, more fundamental changes will be needed to meet the economic, social and environmental dimensions of sustainability; dominant production and consumption patterns will have to change. The final part of the chapter, therefore, sets out the need to create new production systems that will be supportive of the realization of rights, of gender equality and of ecological integrity, through the provisioning of social protection and other public goods and investing in the care economy.

B/ BROADER DEVELOPMENT AND POLICY CONTEXT

Over the past two decades, income inequality has been growing both within and across countries (UNDP, 2013a). The sharpest increases in income inequality have occurred in those developing countries that have been most successful in pursuing vigorous growth strategies that have placed them into higher income brackets (UNDP, 2013a). One of the reasons for this growing inequality has been the changing nature of labour markets. Across a wide range of countries, over the past two to three decades, wage earners have lost out while those relying on profits and rents have increased their relative share of income (International Institute for Labour Studies, 2008; United Nations Conference on Trade and Development (UNCTAD), 2013a; Stockhammer, 2013). At the same time, informal employment continues to be highly prevalent in many parts of the world.[15] Women are more likely than men to be in informal employment, and even within informal employment, men are generally more likely to earn a wage while women are more likely to be in more precarious forms of informal self-employment (Vanek and others, 2014).

The increases in income inequality have been largely driven by processes of globalization, namely, trade and financial liberalization, that have weakened the bargaining position of relatively immobile labour compared to fully mobile capital. But domestic policy choices have also played their part. The experience of a number of developing countries, many of them in Latin America, which have bucked the trend of growing income inequality shows that it is possible to reduce income inequality through economic and social policies while remaining integrated with the global economy (UNDP, 2013a).

Globally too, the distribution of income and wealth remains very unequal. In 2010, high-income countries that accounted for only 16 per cent of the world's population generated close to 55 per cent of global income; low-income countries, by contrast, created just over 1 per cent of global income, even though they were home to 72 per cent of the world's population. The average GDP per capita of $2,014 in sub-Saharan Africa stands in sharp contrast to the average GDP per capita of $27,640 in the European Union and $41,399 in North America (United Nations, 2013b).

Not only is the rise in inequality of concern in terms of its human rights and social implications, it can also have highly adverse economic, environmental and political implications (United Nations, 2013b). For example, high levels of inequality within countries make it harder for societies to reduce poverty through economic growth. Moreover, high levels of inequality, both within and between countries, can in some contexts act as a catalyst for financial crises as a result of underconsumption and the creation of various so-called "bubbles", which can destabilize the economy, as was witnessed in 2008 (Galbraith, 2012; Saith, 2011).

Adding to the social and economic challenges are the risks from another brewing crisis with a global impact, which is likely to reinforce existing inequalities: climate change. The world's poor are especially vulnerable to climate-induced phenomena, including rising sea levels, coastal erosion, storms and desertification. Poorer households and other socially marginalized groups are also among those most likely to lack sufficient clean water, as its availability will increasingly be affected by changing patterns of precipitation, melting glaciers and droughts. Although the causes of these multiple crises vary, they all share a common feature: "in the last two decades much capital has been poured into property, fossil fuels and structured financial assets with embedded derivatives, but relatively little has been invested in renewable energy, energy efficiency, public transportation, sustainable agriculture, and land and water conservation" (UNEP, 2011).

1. Economic and social policy

Macroeconomic policies can have gender-differentiated impacts, as previous issues of the *World Survey* have amply illustrated (see A/54/227; A/64/93).[16] This chapter refers to the sources of gender bias and builds on that analysis by putting the spotlight on the social and environmental dimensions of sustainable development.

The macroeconomic policy agenda that has been dominant over the past three decades is characterized by a core triad of economic liberalization (of both domestic and international markets), macrostability and privatization.[17] Economic liberalization refers to liberalizing domestic markets, including labour and product markets, as well as liberalizing international trade and investment. Trade liberalization has reduced import controls and promoted exports as a promising development strategy and employment generator (UNCTAD, 2010; 2013a). On the investment side, liberalization has been geared towards both foreign direct investment and short-term capital flows. Macrostability is widely understood to mean simply price stability (as opposed to, for instance, employment stability), based on a policy regime, sometimes referred to as deflationary, which tends to weaken the employment-generating capacities of the economy.

With regard to monetary policy, at present, central banks typically try to keep inflation as low as possible by adopting explicit inflation targets. If a low rate of inflation is the only objective, this is likely to lead to higher rates of interest. The result is that the rate of unemployment is kept higher than it would otherwise be. There may be a gender bias to this approach to monetary policy. One empirical analysis, on the basis of data from 17 low- and middle-income countries, assessed

Dominant fiscal policies and public sector reforms constrain the social welfare functions of the state, with negative consequences for social and environmental sustainability. Such dominant policies have focused on cutting back deficit financing of public expenditure and minimizing the tax burden on private enterprises. The emphasis on privatization undermines government action. It is argued that government spending is not only inflationary, but also tends to crowd out private investment. This perspective ignores the fact that public investment can "crowd in" or encourage private investment, for example, when the public provision of infrastructure, education and training, or credit, makes private investment opportunities more attractive. This is especially true in developing economies, where market imperfections are extensive. Public goods are undersupplied by markets relative to what is socially or economically optimal because their social returns are greater than their private returns (Sen, 1999; United Nations, 2013b).

Contractionary monetary policy aimed at reducing inflation often has a disproportionately negative impact on women's employment

the employment outcomes of 51 "inflation reduction episodes" (Braunstein and Heintz, 2008). The study looked at actual employment trends during each inflation reduction episode, disaggregated by gender, and compared these to long-term employment trends. Two significant findings emerged: first, periods of inflation decline are highly likely to be associated with job losses, for both women and men; second, more women than men lose jobs, in percentage terms, when employment contracts. Moreover, in the fewer cases where employment expands during inflation reduction episodes, women do not gain employment faster than men. These results suggest that contractionary monetary policy aimed at reducing inflation often has a disproportionately negative impact on women's employment.

Fiscal constraints that limit the state's capacity to provide public goods often have disproportionately negative impacts on women (and children) in low-income households, partly because of their status in the household and partly because the content of their work is so closely linked with the care economy (Ortiz and Cummins, 2013). This is confirmed by evidence from post-2010 fiscal austerity measures undertaken in a wide range of countries affected by the 2008 global financial crisis, which saw cuts in housing benefits, in child/family allowances, in old age benefits and in care services — cuts that have been disproportionately borne by women (UN-Women, 2014; World Bank, 2012). This perspective also ignores the fact that the public sector has traditionally been an important source of employment, offering women relatively better quality of employment, higher wages and access to pensions and other social benefits (Lund, 2010). Data from ILO confirm that women have historically constituted a significant share of public sector workers in many countries (often higher than their share in total employment) and show that in the countries for which data are available, women constituted 35 per cent of public employees in developing countries, 46 per cent in transition countries and 50 per cent in OECD countries (Hammouya, 1999). Public sector downsizing has led to a disproportionate impact on formal employment opportunities for women and is likely to increase women's concentration in less formal, non-regular jobs (Lee, 2005).

Turning from social to environmental sustainability, the diminished social welfare functions of the state also produce and reinforce vulnerability to climate change (Fieldman, 2011). The inadequacy of state provisioning of infrastructure, services and social protection means that measures for adaptation or building resilience to climate change that take into account gender equality and social justice, such as investments in flood defences or research on drought-resistant seeds, remain under-funded. The state's capacity to regulate, manage and tax a broad range of policy areas related to the environment in order to finance effective conservation efforts is thus vital (UNDP, 2011).

Taken together, the macro policy conventions of liberalization, privatization and macrostability create a deflationary economic environment characterized by reduced capacity to generate employment, fiscal squeeze and limited public policy space, with implications for the achievement of social and environmental sustainability. In such a context, it may appear that the best, or indeed the only, avenue for generating employment and raising incomes is to pursue an export-led growth strategy. But, in the past decade or so, two new economic developments have emerged that make pursuing such an externally-oriented agenda even more complex. First, as more countries shift to production for export markets, competition between producers

in far-flung corners of the world has intensified. This in turn has exerted pressure on wages and wage-related entitlements, especially in labour-intensive sectors such as garments, apparel and electronics, which employ significant numbers of women (Seguino, 2000). As a result, the achievement of a decent work agenda necessary for social sustainability is compromised. The shift of production processes to developing countries also relocates the ecological and health costs of polluting production processes to countries with less stringent environmental regulations (UNCTAD, 2013b). The second recent development concerns intensified global imbalances, which threaten the economic sustainability of the model, to which the chapter now turns.

2. Inequality and economic unsustainability

Rising levels of income inequality are contributing to the unsustainability of the dominant economic model, even on its own limited terms. For some countries, the long-term decline in savings and the accumulation of private debt has increased consumption in spite of stagnant earnings, resulting in large current account deficits. At the same time, countries with a current account surplus used export markets as a way to sustain employment in the absence of sufficient domestic aggregate demand (Blecker, 2012; UNCTAD, 2010). The collective result was a state of underconsumption in some regions and overborrowing in others, financed in part by global financial flows from current account surplus countries to deficit countries. This process was further facilitated by the rising tide of financialization[18] and the shift in emphasis from production to financial profit-making (Cripps, Izurieta and Singh, 2011).

Such terms of production and exchange are economically unsustainable and have led to global imbalances,[19] which played an important role in the recent global economic crisis (Bernanke, 2011; UNCTAD, 2010). Although global imbalances did not set off the financial crisis of 2007-2008, they helped transmit its contagion. While the particular national circumstances of these imbalances differed, they all produced a trajectory of wage growth that lagged far behind productivity growth and resulted in rising levels of inequality across both the global North and South (Blecker, 2012). They demonstrate the systemic paradox of relying on exports coupled with wage stagnation to deliver growth and development.

Developed countries, for the most part, continue to exhibit sluggish growth and high unemployment as many governments wield austerity-type policies in the hope of reducing deficits and restoring economic confidence. In developing countries, the most affected by the global crisis were emerging market economies with current account deficits that could not withstand the drop in capital inflows resulting from the crisis (UNCTAD, 2010). But for low-income countries that had little involvement with global capital markets, and for countries with current account surpluses and/or substantial international reserves, the negative impact of the financial crisis has been shorter lived and less severe. For instance, many Asian and Latin American countries employed counter-cyclical monetary and fiscal policies, turning towards domestic sources of demand to counter declines in global trade (UNRISD, 2010). These countries have in fact led the global recovery, but the re-emergence of growth, trade and employment generation is far from complete (World Bank, 2014). In significant ways, there has been a shift of global production and consumption to large emerging economies, which in turn has helped smaller economies that cannot rely on their own domestic demand by providing new markets for export (Gereffi, 2014; UNCTAD, 2013a).

However, the rise of emerging economies is not nearly sufficient to launch a renewed era of export-led growth opportunities. While it is true that emerging market economies have added to global demand, the issue is one of scale and structure. In terms of scale, for instance, demand from middle-income countries is a very long way from replacing that of large developed countries as the global engine of consumption growth (Cripps, Izurieta and Singh, 2011). In terms of structure, a shift away from demand in industrialized countries means a shift away from demand for manufactured goods to a demand for raw materials, energy and food, while the latter also figure more prominently in the demand of emerging market economies. This shift in demand towards raw materials, energy and food has consequences for global commodity prices, which will increase, as well as for terms of trade, whereby countries with labour-intensive manufacturing will buy fewer imports (UNCTAD, 2010).

Restoring growth and jobs on the basis of the "brown economy", with its dependence on low-energy efficiency and non-sustainable energy sources is deeply problematic. In the immediate post-crisis period, stimulus packages that were allocated to restoring the automobile industry, rather than investing in public transport and renewable energy sources, were a source of concern. Such investments risk reproducing the imbalances and vulnerabilities that caused the multiple crises, rather than using the crisis as an opportunity to steer economies and societies along more sustainable pathways. There has been increasing public awareness that current consumption patterns are depleting key natural resources and placing unsustainable burdens on the planet's ecosystem. There is an urgent need for discussing, designing and adopting policies to establish clear resource and environmental limits and integrate these into economic and social systems (Jackson, 2011).

There is an urgent need for discussing, designing and adopting policies to establish clear resource and environmental limits and integrate these into economic and social systems

C/ SEARCHING FOR ALTERNATIVES: GREEN ECONOMY AND GENDER EQUALITY

Given the unsustainability of global imbalances and the limited prospects for a renewed era of export-led growth, it is important to consider what rebalancing should look like. In its *Trade and Development Report* (2010), UNCTAD essentially argues for two things: first, high-income countries with current account surpluses need to turn away from export dependence and start importing, implementing policies that encourage wage and consumption growth; and second, a global macro policy shift is needed towards a growth regime that is led by wages and supports the expansion of domestic aggregate demand. For smaller or low-income economies with insufficiently large domestic markets, exporting to a wider variety of importers, or trading within regional blocs where the old model of global export dominance no longer holds sway, will serve as supplemental engines of growth and development.

It is not clear if rebalancing the global economy along the lines proposed by UNCTAD (2010), through the expansion of domestic demand, would improve the prospects for women's employment. There is some work to suggest that expanding domestic sources of aggregate demand enables a rise in female wages and a decline in the gender wage gap without sacrificing economic growth (Blecker and Seguino, 2002; Seguino and Grown, 2006). Furthermore, given the association between women's income and spending on basic needs, there may also be positive ripple effects for domestic production to the extent that demand shifts away from imports (Benería and Roldán, 1987; Blumberg, 1991; Haddad, Hoddinott and Alderman, 1997). The issue of the balance of payment constraints remains, however, if there

is a shift from more export-oriented strategies to greater reliance on domestic demand. It is possible that improvements in capabilities that are a consequence of higher incomes for women, will compensate for the loss in foreign exchange a scenario that is more likely in low-income agricultural economies than in semi-industrialized ones (Seguino, 2010).

A further important consideration is whether a demand-led growth model would be better for environmental sustainability. The answer would hinge on the kind of demand that is encouraged: for example, demand that is characterized by consumption of low-carbon and climate-resilient goods and services is very different from one that is based on fossil fuels and natural resource extraction. As such, pursuing a shift to demand-led growth, on its own, is unlikely to address the environmental costs associated with sustained growth, unless the higher wages and earnings of lower income groups that will result from such a shift are spent on goods that are less reliant on fossil fuels and natural resource extraction, and increased public expenditure and investment is also allocated to fuel-efficient sectors and technologies. This is where proposals for green economy become relevant.

1. Green economy

The environmental and social costs associated with dominant patterns of growth have motivated the search for alternative models of development that are sustainable. A case in point is the green economy agenda, where the greening of investment and public policy in both developing and developed countries is intended to enhance environmental protection while also creating jobs and stimulating economic growth (ILO, 2012; UNCTAD, 2013a). There are, however, different variants of green economy.

Dominant variants of green economy assume continued, even enhanced, market-led economic growth, through green business investments and innovations that increase energy and resource efficiency and prevent the loss of ecosystem services. Other strands emphasize market-based approaches to environmental protection through financial valuation of natural capital (e.g., Natural Capital Committee, 2013), payments for ecosystem services and schemes for trading carbon and biodiversity credits and offsets. For the proponents of such approaches, markets fail to price natural assets and ecosystem services, which are ultimately factors of production much like capital and labour. The result is that this natural capital is overexploited relative to what is socially or economically optimal. In this context, where negative externalities render market outcomes socially inefficient, market interventions, such as taxing carbon or legislating so that forest management rights are given to local communities, are aimed at properly pricing natural assets and defining property rights. In doing so, they bring market-determined growth processes more closely in line with environmental values (World Bank, 2012).

These market-based approaches can be problematic from a social perspective, leading to greater inequality and injustice for local users vis-à-vis external and global actors. As a recent report by the United Nations Research Institute for Social Development (UNRISD) puts it, payments for ecological services, the process relating to the United Nations Collaborative Programme on Reducing Emissions from Deforestation and Forest Degradation in Developing Countries (REDD) and incentives to produce biofuels often involve trade-offs with smallholder agriculture, biodiversity, livelihoods and food security. Moreover, market-based approaches often promote corporate interests, which in turn may constrain the scope for policy and regulatory reform that is conducive to social and sustainable development (UNRISD, 2012b).

As such, there is not enough integration of the social dimensions of sustainable development in these market-based approaches to green economy.

A green economy, according to UNEP, is one that ends extreme poverty, improves human well-being and enhances social equity while reducing carbon dependency and ecosystem degradation and furthering sustainable and inclusive growth (UNEP, 2009; 2011). This definition corresponds to the general understanding of sustainable development and its three dimensions, economic, social and environmental. Green Keynesianism, also presented as green stimulus or a "global green new deal" (GGND), argues for directing government spending towards technology and employment generation in ways that enhance environmental protection and raise efficiency, for instance by retrofitting energy-inefficient buildings or infrastructure (e.g., UNEP, 2009). These sorts of green investments were a much-discussed and promoted part of countercyclical macroeconomic policies adopted in the wake of the global recession of 2008, in both developed and developing countries. The proposal by UNEP emphasized the principle of common but differentiated responsibilities with regard to developed countries, emerging economies, countries with economies in transition and the least developed countries. A "fair and just GGND, therefore, should consider including developed countries' additional support to other countries, especially least developed countries, in the areas of finance, trade, technology and capacity building in the interest of effectiveness as well as fairness" (UNEP, 2009). Gender equality is a marginal concern in most of these proposals.

An alternative to the green economy approaches discussed above is the work of those linked with the environmental justice movements, who see environmental preservation as an opportunity to understand and redress multiple forms of inequality. For example, maintaining crop biodiversity enables future food producers to deal with new pests and diseases that threaten the food supply. Today, crop biodiversity is sustained largely by farmers in the global

South, but they receive no compensation for this tremendously valuable social and ecological service (Boyce, 2011). Compensating farmers in the global South for their contributions to long-term food security should appeal to green economy advocates, but it also directly addresses questions of development and sustainability in economically just and pro-poor ways. Explicitly incorporating women's traditional work in agriculture, for example, in seed selection and preservation to maintain crop biodiversity, is important in these analyses. Moreover, gender inequality in land rights and access to resources, as well as in the burden of unpaid care work, poses substantial barriers to greening agriculture in sustainable and pro-poor ways (Herren and others, 2012).

2. Women and green jobs

A part of the green growth agenda targets the expansion of green jobs, which are understood primarily in terms of their environmental impact, but also seek to comply with ILO notions of decent work (International Labour Foundation for Sustainable Development, 2009; ILO, 2012; UNEP and others, 2008).[20] In terms of industry, where it is estimated that 80 per cent of green jobs will be located, a small number of manufacturing industries are responsible for a large share of resource and energy use as well as greenhouse gas emissions and other pollutants (International Labour Foundation for Sustainable Development, 2009). These include energy, construction, transportation and, among basic industries, aluminium, iron and steel (ILO, 2012).

Most of the projected employment gains are expected to come from activities involved in transitioning to a low-carbon economy, including developing renewable energy resources, producing more fuel-efficient vehicles, constructing and retrofitting buildings, transport and infrastructure, and waste management and recycling. In manufacturing, the emphasis is on introducing clean processing techniques and controlling pollution, with less of an apparent total employment effect (International Labour Foundation for Sustainable Development, 2009).

Green jobs are generally middle-skill jobs, and expanding sectors are seen as more skill- and knowledge-intensive than their counterparts in conventional industry; the concomitant pay and benefits are also higher (Chan and Ching Lam, 2012; Muro and others, 2011). These features make the association between green jobs and decent work a seemingly natural one, but the connection is closer in some sectors than others. Investments in agriculture, for example, which continues to be the single largest sector in terms of employment, and which is the main sector of employment in rural areas, where the majority of the world's poor and extremely poor live and work, are potentially very promising. The shift to green jobs is also sometimes seen as an opportunity to draw women into non-traditional, more highly paid sectors such as engineering, construction and manufacturing because they are perceived as less limited by entrenched gender stereotypes (International Labour Foundation for Sustainable Development, 2009).

Though the goals of greening jobs are laudable, benefits for women may not be automatic and the potential impacts on women's employment requires explicit consideration. Given the extent of gender segregation in labour markets generally, and within industry in particular, where women constitute only 30 per cent of the global workforce, there is a risk that efforts to green industry will not only bypass women, but actually marginalize them. Sectors targeted for green employment expansion, such as energy, construction and basic industry, are very male-dominated and recent trends indicate that sectoral segregation is increasing rather than decreasing.[21] Among green jobs that already exist, women tend to have low representation and/or occupy the lower value-added rungs. For instance, in OECD countries, where women earn more than half of university degrees, only 30 per cent of degrees in science and technology (key areas of study for green jobs) go to women. In developing economies, women are highly concentrated on the low value-added end of extant green jobs, for instance as informal workers in waste collection and recycling (Strietska-Ilina and others, 2011).

Envisioning environmentally sustainable industrial transformation means targeting specific skill development and education for women, as well as ensuring equal pay and the elimination of workplace discrimination, as part of the broader decent work agenda (ILO, 2012; International Labour Foundation for Sustainable Development, 2009; UNEP and others, 2008). Efforts to break down stereotypes are also necessary. Gender stereotyping takes place from an early age and is pervasive across society: at home, in schools, in the media and through day-to-day social attitudes and interactions which embed and reinforce them. This contributes to the clustering of women and men into different subject areas in secondary school and higher education. As various studies have shown, the low representation of women in science, technology, engineering and mathematics is related to attitudes rather than ability: girls, for example, do not receive lower scores in mathematics. Even though differences in occupational choices can be traced back to subjects studied, occupational segregation between women and men is further reinforced in the transition from post-secondary education to employment. In OECD countries, for example, even if women choose science, technology, engineering and mathematics as subjects, they are less likely than men to pursue a career in science, although there is no gender difference in performance (Organization for Economic Cooperation and Development (OECD), 2012).

There are several examples of green jobs that have included women. For example, in the "Working for Water" project in South Africa, a part of its expanded public works programme that trained people to remove invasive alien plants in order to enhance water access, ultimately successful efforts were made to specifically recruit women, youth and people with disabilities to take part in the project (Strietska-Ilina and others, 2011). In Bangladesh, as part of a larger project to extend electricity to rural areas by installing solar home systems, women were trained to install and repair solar panels and electrical outlets, serving as "rural electricians" in ways that are revolutionary by

traditional labour market standards (ILO, 2012; Sidner, 2011). In the United States of America, a number of programmes aim to encourage women into green jobs through skill development and networking, including the Women in Apprenticeship and Non-traditional Occupations programme, which gives grants to community-based organizations that provide openings for women into non-traditional occupations, such as pre apprenticeship programmes, with recent rounds emphasizing green jobs.

While these efforts are instructive and promising, they do not directly address structural inequalities associated with the low wages, poor working conditions and precarious livelihoods of large numbers of women and men who are beyond the reach of these innovative but small-scale initiatives. Some of this promise can be seen in the case of waste pickers, where efforts for greening work have gone beyond patchy skill development to address informality and marginalization.

In developed countries, the waste management and recycling industries are highly formalized and automated, and they are dominated by men. But in developing and emerging economies, an estimated 15 to 20 million waste pickers, many of them women and children, driven into this work by poverty, reclaim reusable and recyclable materials from what others have discarded, providing an essential environmental service in areas experiencing rapid urbanization with limited public services (ILO, 2012; Samson, 2009). The work is largely informal, the earnings low and unstable, and it is typically associated with strong social stigma and very poor, even hazardous working conditions (ILO, 2012). For example, 20-50 million tons of electronic waste, containing valuable metals, are discarded each year, with much of the discarded equipment exported to countries such as China and India for dismantling. The materials often go to small, informal family workshops or other informal facilities to be processed, where knowledge is limited and dangers are high (ILO, 2012). However, the contributions waste pickers make to social and environmental sustainability are

Organizing benefits waste pickers by raising their social status and self-esteem, as well as their incomes

substantial: they improve public health and sanitation; divert materials from the waste stream; reduce the need to use new materials; provide very cost-efficient waste management systems for municipalities; and provide livelihoods for the poor and marginalized.22

Efforts to organize and enfranchise waste pickers worldwide, both among the waste pickers themselves and with help from global institutions such as ILO, provide a useful example of using green jobs as a channel for greater social inclusion (ILO, 2012). Women are more likely than men to participate in organizations for waste pickers, perhaps because they tend to be concentrated in lower-earning waste-picking activities, and are typically paid lower rates than men for equivalent work. Organizing benefits waste pickers by raising their social status and

self-esteem, as well as their incomes. Organized waste pickers are better able to circumvent middlemen and negotiate fair prices for their materials from buyers. Collectively, they are also better able to prevent harassment and violence. There are also attempts to better incorporate waste pickers into waste management and recycling value chains, countering the push towards commercialization, which is linked with incineration and landfill technologies. These attempts instead promote zero waste strategies that maximize recycling and provide decent employment for the poor (ILO, 2012). Examples of such efforts abound in all regions of the world, with most focused on expanding the social power and safety that comes with collective organization, legalizing and formalizing relationships with municipalities and increasing access to social protections.

D/ ALTERNATIVE RESPONSES TO UNSUSTAINABILITY: INVESTING IN PUBLIC GOODS AND THE CARE ECONOMY

A gender-responsive green economy that enhances women's employment prospects and the quality of their work along the lines of the decent work agenda is an important step towards addressing both social sustainability and

gender inequality. But it is not sufficient. In order to redress gender inequality and promote the three dimensions of sustainable development, policymakers need to pay attention to investments in public goods and the care economy.

© Deia de Brito

Nohra Padilla, a waste picker since the age of 7, organizer, and activist from Bogota has brought the struggle for livelihood rights for waste pickers to the global stage. She was awarded the Goldman Environmental Award in 2013. Here Nohra is speaking to waste pickers from around the world at the First Global Workshop of Waste Pickers in Pune, India

Since the crisis of 2007-2008, there have been important calls for the reform of the global financial system. But there is growing recognition that not only will the global financial system have to be changed in order for economies to meet the economic, social and environmental dimensions of sustainability, but dominant production and consumption patterns will also have to change. "Measures to end the crisis will fail if they simply seek to restore growth and greed" (Elson, 2011). More sophisticated criteria than simple GDP measures will need to be developed in order to assess success.

Measures to end the crisis will fail if they simply seek to restore growth and greed

There are calls for an ecological macroeconomics, the starting point of which must be to abandon the presumption of perpetual consumption growth as the only basis for economic stability and to identify the conditions that define a sustainable economy, including strong resilience to external shocks and avoiding internal contradictions, which create social tensions during recessions; secure livelihoods with equality; and sustainable levels of resource use that protect the ecosystem (Jackson, 2011).

Across the world, an increase in privately produced and consumed goods and services, rather than the increase in the enjoyment of human rights, expanded capabilities and well-being, has been used as the hallmark of success. Women, too, have been encouraged to understand gender equality and empowerment in terms of being able to buy more consumer goods (Elson, 2011). It is frequently assumed that policymakers should first try to maximize the economic pie (GDP), and then address issues of equality, well-being and justice by redistributing the pie. Another assumption is that the best

way to create wealth is through production by privately owned, profit-seeking businesses operating in markets that are regulated in ways that promote competition between such businesses. The human rights- and capability-based approaches have a different aim, which is the expansion of people's substantive choices to live a life they have reason to value. This means being able to enjoy a richer set of rights, far beyond the utility that would come from consuming more. It would include the right to be free from poverty and hunger, the right to health and social security, and the right to participate in decisions that affect one's life.

Feminist economics shares many of the values of the human rights and capability approaches, but it places a particular emphasis on an economic and social system that includes not only paid work but also non-market unpaid care work (Grown, Elson and Cagatay, 2000). Most mainstream economic approaches that inform policymaking tend to privilege production for the market. The sphere of unpaid work is taken for granted. Feminist economics challenges this exclusion, arguing that as well as the economy of the market and the state, policymakers need to take into account the unpaid economy in which people produce goods and services for their families, friends and neighbours on the basis of social obligation, altruism and reciprocity, and in some cases, coercion. In this unpaid economy, people produce food and clothing, fetch fuel and water, cook and clean, and take care of others, especially children, frail elderly people and those who are sick (Elson, 1998; 2011; Folbre, 1994; 2001; UNDP, 1995; UNRISD, 2010). There are two reasons for underscoring the centrality of the unpaid economy for policymaking: first, because it makes a fundamental contribution to people's well-being, which is critical for social sustainability; and second, even though unpaid care is not adequately measured through statistics and taken into account in policymaking, it affects the operation of other parts of the economy, including private firms (large and small), the public sector and the non-governmental sector, by affecting the quantity and quality of labour needed to run these entities; as such, it creates the foundation for economic sustainability (Elson, 1998; 2011). These alternative ways of thinking about economic success and failure direct attention to two sets of issues that are fundamental for policymaking.

First, policymakers need to address the issue of how people can be guaranteed the exercise of their human rights and capabilities (to be well-nourished, healthy, literate, able to take part in the life of the community) when the resources they obtain through their existing entitlement relations, through paid work or subsistence agriculture for example, are not sufficient. The insufficiency of their market-based earnings may be as a result of working in low-paid sectors of the economy, or having unpaid care obligations that do not allow them to earn an adequate income, or attributable to not owning capital or land that would generate sufficient earnings from self-employment. But there are also structural factors that often explain such entitlement failures: for example, highly unequal and discriminatory property relations that prevent significant numbers of people, especially women, from accessing land and other productive assets; and high levels of structural unemployment, underemployment and informality that do not allow people, in particular women, to realize their right to work and their rights at work.

In response to such failures in recent years, policymakers in different parts of the world have directed their attention to social security systems.[23] Many useful lessons have been learned from the narrowly targeted safety nets of the early 1990s that aimed to identify the needy through various means tests: in the context of weak administrative capacity, means tests can be administratively costly; inadequate information about household circumstances adds to this complexity and can exclude the poor (through so-called errors of omission); social assistance measures need to be institutionalized, rather than ad hoc measures, and financed where possible through a robust tax-and-transfer system; and in contexts of pervasive poverty, broad-based and universal systems can be more accessible, more transparent and more effective than narrowly targeted measures (Mkandawire, 2005; UNRISD, 2010; Sepúlveda and Nyst, 2012).

Indeed, the need for social security systems that are responsive to changing circumstances is now more urgent than ever, as recognized by the Social Protection Floor Initiative. Recurring and multiple crises have highlighted the importance of social protection as a buffer against sudden drops in income and employment. In addition, rapid rates of urbanization, changes in family and household structures, demographic transitions, migration and health crises of various kinds call for innovative approaches that are able to protect people and help them adjust in the face of new challenges. In doing so, social protection measures can bolster the realization of economic and social rights, but also foster economic development and transformation (UNRISD, 2010).

However, the potential of social protection measures is still far from being realized. Only 27 per cent of the world's population enjoys access to comprehensive social security, whereas 73 per cent are covered partially or not at all (ILO, 2014). Similarly, it is estimated that about one third of the global population lacks access to any health care, and for an even greater share, health costs are a major burden and an important factor pushing households into poverty and indebtedness. Progress on the attendance of girls at secondary school, the number of births assisted by skilled health professionals and access to improved water sources and sanitation facilities has also been mixed. While many countries have seen significant improvements in these indicators over the past two decades, access among lower-income women and girls lags well behind that of higher-income women and girls (United Nations, 2013b). Disturbingly, inequalities between women from different income groups have widened rather than narrowed in a number of countries (Elson, 2014).

Women are disproportionately affected, and in different ways, by the lack of access to social security and social services, compared to men (Razavi and Hassim, 2006). Gender inequality is particularly visible in contexts where public provision is weak, since women's more constrained access to income, savings and assets means that they are less likely to be able to access private insurance schemes and are more affected by user fees for social services. The absence of adequate public support also reinforces the reliance on informal social security systems. Dependence on kinship and community networks can be deeply problematic from a gender perspective. On the one hand, these networks usually rely, to a significant degree, on women's unpaid care work. On the other hand, prevailing social norms and gender power relations in households and communities may limit the extent to which women's own needs are acknowledged and addressed.

Greater state involvement does not in and of itself resolve these problems. Examples abound of gender gaps in access to public social security and gender-blind social service delivery. In some contexts, social security and services are delivered in ways that marginalize, stigmatize or overburden women, especially those from poor, ethnic minority, disabled and indigenous backgrounds (Sepúlveda and Nyst, 2012). As a result, women's enjoyment of basic human rights, including the right to an adequate standard of living, is severely hampered. Greater state involvement in the regulation, financing and provision of social goods is not a sufficient condition for substantive gender equality. From a human rights perspective, the state is the duty bearer that must guarantee the enjoyment of human rights. The human rights system underscores the positive duties of the state to respect, protect and fulfil rights.[24] These principles have been used by the Committee on Economic, Social and Cultural Rights, in its General Comments on specific rights including the rights to education; health; water; work; and social security.[25]

The second element that needs policy attention is the system of production and consumption. It is important to critically examine the dominant systems of production and to create new

production systems that will be supportive of the realization of rights, of gender equality and of ecological integrity.

An important element of this alternative production system is the need to pay far greater attention to social production, investment and consumption (Elson, 2011). This would mean production by for-profit as well as non-profit institutions such as cooperatives and community enterprises, community management of forest and irrigation systems, as well as community kitchens and childcare centres. While states may be active in some of these arrangements, they would not be the only actors. The advantage of these hybrid systems is that they can be responsive to the needs and demands of all, irrespective of income or wealth. "It is often argued that private production is more responsive to consumer demand, but the response is only to consumers with enough money" (Elson, 2011). It is important that social production responds not only to the rights and interests of producers but also to the rights of users. This would require the strengthening of rights of users and building direct links between producers and users.

Social production and investment are vital to ensure a sufficient quantity of public goods, that is to say goods whose benefits spill over to those who do not directly utilize them: education, public health, good public transport systems, water and sanitation and clean energy systems. It is now increasingly recognized that a sustainable climate is an important public good. What is not sufficiently recognized is that a sustainable care system is also an important public good (Folbre, 2001). Much of this care is provided on an unpaid basis (Budlender, 2010). But paid care services also make up a growing part of the economy and of employment in many countries, especially of women's employment (Razavi and Staab, 2010).[26] The availability of care services, whether these are provided through households and communities on an unpaid basis, or through markets and the public sector which employ care workers, is essential for the well-being of all persons. When care work is decently paid and protected, it can meet the interests of both care workers and users of services. It can also reduce the burden that is placed on women and girls in their role as unpaid carers.

To date, the care economy has been largely isolated from the ongoing policy debates on the green economy. Part of the problem lies in how economists think about growth. By the standards of a typical growth model, the

addition to their added value, are both labour-intensive and traditional sources of employment for women, and so offer the potential to increase women's employment.

Governments are increasingly recognizing this potential. In the Republic of Korea, for example, since 2000, the government has significantly expanded social care provision in the form of universal long-term insurance schemes for the elderly and publicly subsidized childcare.

When care work is decently paid and protected, it can meet the interests of both care workers and users of services

process of development is simply a process of accumulation of capital and growth in productivity. Though most contemporary growth models incorporate some measure of human as well as physical capital, human capital is rarely treated as a component of investment.[27] And while growth prescriptions almost always call for investment in skills, such calls are limited to increasing formal education. This approach to growth and development ignores the significant amount of unpaid and paid care work that goes into sustaining people from day to day and from one generation to the next.

One way for policy to support the care economy is by shifting towards more care-intensive or social services-intensive activities, which would also have environmental benefits, since providing care does not generally entail intensive use of environmental resources (Jackson, 2011). The service sector is the largest employer of both women and men in high-income countries, and an increasingly important contributor to productivity growth in developing economies. The service sector, however, is highly uneven. Higher value-added services (e.g., information and communications technology) tend to generate very little employment relative to their added value in emerging economies (UNCTAD, 2010). Care-related services, in

These and other social policy measures, such as statutory parental leave, which were adopted to support the care economy, are seen as an engine for economic growth by redistributing care responsibilities more equally between state, market, family and community (Peng, 2012).

Another example is Pakistan's "Lady health worker" programme, which establishes a vital link between households and health services, particularly for women in rural areas, whose mobility is restricted. The programme is also a major employer of women in a country where employment opportunities for women are rather limited. The women who are recruited undergo training from a qualified doctor at the closest primary health-care centre for 15 months. They can then work from home, where they attend to community members, hold meetings and store basic medicines, including contraceptives. Lady health workers work an average of 30 hours per week. The programme is an important source of regular and predictable income for these women. It also offers women expanded mobility and enhances the visibility and credibility of working women (Khan, 2014). As such, it can be seen as a catalyst of positive change and a source of empowerment through the state-sponsored expansion of health-care employment. It is important to note, however, that these workers earn less than the national minimum wage.

The experience of Pakistan's lady health workers, in terms of pay, is far from unique. The care sector is characterized by relatively low earnings and exacts what is termed a "care penalty" in pay. The care penalty refers to the systematically lower wages that care workers receive compared with wages for non-care jobs that require similar levels of skill and education (Budig and Misra, 2010; England, Budig and Folbre, 2002). Comparing the salaries of primary teachers and nurses in more than 20 developing countries reveals that in 2009, many were near the poverty line (Chai, Ortiz and Sire, 2010). The terms and conditions of employment for care sector workers need to be better regulated and improved (Folbre, 2006). This requires effective regulation and monitoring by states, but also a critical role to be played by the organizations of care workers and of care-users, who need to build public confidence in such services and sustain their adequate financing.

Raising women's employment in service sector occupations, especially care related services, must include policies that address overall gender segregation in labour markets and the relatively low pay of such workers. The absence of such policies risks confining women to a few occupations and exacerbating occupational segregation. Therefore, public investment in the care sector needs to be accompanied by policies that reduce occupational and sectoral segregation and improve the pay and labour market conditions of such work so that women have an expanding range of options open to them. To be truly sustainable, an economic strategy that is responsive to care needs and to gender equality must also be concerned with making care work decent work. It falls on the state to lead the shift from a strategy that relies on market-based and "voluntary" provision of care that is of the most informal and exploitative kind, to one that nurtures professional forms of care with decent pay (UNRISD, 2010).

One important step towards this is the Domestic Workers Convention, 2011 (No. 189) of the International Labour Organization. The convention, which entered into force in September 2013, for the first time in history extends basic labour rights to an estimated 53 million domestic workers, 83 per cent of whom are women, many of them belonging to racial or ethnic minorities (ILO, 2013). To date, 14 countries have ratified the convention and it has entered into force in nine of those countries. While increasing ratifications is clearly a priority, it is important to acknowledge that other countries have also taken important steps to regulate domestic work and ensure decent pay and conditions for these vulnerable workers. In Namibia, unlike in many countries, domestic workers are covered by labour legislation and they have the same rights to employment protection, weekly rest and maternity leave (ILO, 2013). However, enforcement of these rights remains a challenge. In response to this and in order to move closer to ratification of the Convention, the Government of Namibia set up a Wages Commission in 2012 to recommend a new minimum wage for domestic workers and investigate other conditions of work (Hammerton, 2013).

There are some common elements between environmental services and care services. Both exist primarily outside of the traditional market sphere, but they are increasingly commodified and their market valuation is far from an accurate reflection of their social value. In a related sense, they are public goods with positive externalities that make the market mechanism an economically inefficient arbiter of their use. As a result of these market failures, both human and natural resources are in danger of being overexploited, given the incentives produced by the prevailing global economic system.

These parallels point to the need for state action, both in terms of regulating markets in ways that more equitably and accurately price the social value of ecosystem services and care, and as regards social provisioning of and investment in infrastructure and services that reflect their nature as public goods. Barring such intervention, market operations will result in shortages of ecological and care services, shortages that ultimately press into the realm of crisis.

E/ BROADENING THE GREEN ECONOMY AGENDA

The dominant development models present formidable challenges for social, environmental and even economic sustainability, as the multiple crises of recent years have made clear. Current economic models have been limited in reducing gender inequalities and enabling the realization of human rights. Policymakers need to steer their economies and societies along new pathways, within which sustainability and gender equality can reinforce each other. In order to do so, policies should be aimed at the creation of green jobs that offer decent pay and working conditions and provide social protection and prospects for advancement, within an enabling macroeconomic framework policy.

Current efforts to promote green jobs often overlook the potential, in the context of creating a green economy, of providing decent work and sustainable livelihoods for women. If green jobs schemes are to expand their scope and

impact, they need to become more inclusive of women and more gender-responsive. This means ensuring that green growth policies increase access for women, particularly poor and marginalized women, into high quality jobs in sustainable and low-carbon industries. The potential of integrating the green and care economies remains largely untapped, but if properly resourced and supported, would constitute an important strategy for achieving economic, social and environmental sustainability.

In order for this strategy to advance gender equality and human rights, the expansion of women's capabilities and the recognition, reduction and redistribution of care would have to become key criteria for policy success. Moving away from current patterns of consumption and production requires an emphasis on social investment, production and consumption through hybrid systems involving for-profit as well as a variety of non-profit institutions that can be responsive to people's needs and demands, irrespective of their income or wealth. A key priority would be investments in a variety of public goods, including health, education, food, water and sanitation and sustainable energy, as well as robust and gender-responsive care systems to ensure social sustainability.

If green jobs schemes are to expand their scope and impact, they need to become more inclusive of women and more gender-responsive

CHAPTER /4

FOOD SECURITY AND GENDER EQUALITY

A/ INTRODUCTION

Achieving food security is a central part of sustainable development, across the three dimensions. The ability of people to realize their right to food, to feed themselves, is essential today, but so is the capacity of future generations to be able to exercise their right to food. Ensuring an end to malnutrition and hunger requires a focus on agriculture and food production systems both in their relationship with natural resources on the one hand, and with global and national economic structures and policies, on the other. Achieving that goal also requires analysis of the context-specific social relations, including unequal gender power relations that constrain access to food by individuals and households.

The problems of hunger and malnutrition have recaptured the attention of world leaders since the food crisis of 2007 onwards, but the challenges have their roots in both long-term and short-term policy failures. This chapter is concerned with food security as an essential aspect of sustainable development, with gender equality at its core, because to be free from hunger is a human right, and to be adequately nourished is a basic capability without which many other opportunities for a fulfilling life cannot be seized. In particular, women's and girls' right to food and nutrition must be supported.

The right to food was first recognized in the Universal Declaration of Human Rights (General Assembly resolution 217 A (III)), adopted in 1948, and later elaborated in the International Covenant on Economic, Social and Cultural Rights (see General Assembly resolution 2200 A (XXI), annex). The International Covenant reaffirms the right to food and the important elements of availability, accessibility and utilization, as well as the fundamental right of everyone to be free from hunger. In its General Comment No. 12, the Committee on Economic, Social and Cultural Rights explained the normative content of the right to adequate food (article 11 of the Covenant). It underscored, among other elements, the importance of cultural appropriateness, nutritional adequacy and sustainability of access, and outlined the obligations of states and the international community in reinforcing the right to food (see E/2000/22 and Corr.1, annex V, General Comment No. 12).

The definition of food security that was adopted at the World Food Summit, in 1996,[10] reflects the need to prioritize access and asserts that food security exists when all people, at all times, have physical and economic access to sufficient safe and nutritious food that meets their dietary needs and food preferences for an active and healthy life. The four components or pillars of food security include the availability of food; economic, physical and social access to food; food utilization; and the stability of these three dimensions over time. The outcome document of the United Nations Conference on Sustainable Development further reinforces the right to food (General Assembly resolution 66/288, annex, para. 108) and highlights "the necessity to promote, enhance and support more sustainable agriculture, including crops, livestock, forestry, fisheries and aquaculture, that improves food security, eradicates hunger and is economically viable, while conserving land, water, plant and animal genetic resources, biodiversity and ecosystems and enhancing resilience to climate change and natural disasters" (resolution 66/288, annex, para. 111).

Though substantial progress has been made in reducing the incidence of hunger and malnutrition over the past two decades, current trends in food consumption and production raise concerns about the prospects for achieving sustainable food security. Undernutrition and malnutrition persist in old forms, while new forms are also on the rise. Climate change and environmental degradation affect food production, especially for the most food-insecure households. While competition regarding land use for biofuels, along with new financial instruments, contribute to price volatility in global markets for cereals, increased demand for farmland from foreign investors risks disrupting the access of smallholders and pastoralists to land for sustaining their livelihoods.

Current debates about priority investments to combat hunger and malnutrition are framed as a problem of imbalances between production and population, or global shortages, rather than the inability of individuals to acquire food that is of adequate quantity and quality. A broad array of national and global policy actors and researchers have called for a 70 per cent increase in food production by 2050 in order to feed the estimated world population of 9 billion people. The focus is on global aggregates rather than the situation of countries and subnational groups. This approach dominates popular as well as academic and public policy debates and explains hunger as a problem of production shortages, attributable to such factors as overpopulation, war and drought, to which climate change and increasing biofuel production are adding new pressures (Tomlinson, 2013).

Food production is clearly an essential element of food security, but it is not the only one. As Amartya Sen pointed out more than three decades ago, hunger is about "people not having enough food to eat. It is not the characteristic of there not being enough food

to eat" (Sen, 1982). Food security depends on access. In the context of climate change and environmental degradation, access to food for both food producers and food purchasers may become more constrained. A policy agenda on food security must be based on an analysis of the constraints to the acquisition of food of adequate quality and quantity. Food security must be considered a public good, the provision of which states must ensure in the context of an enabling international environment.

Gender analysis is important for understanding the causes of hunger and malnutrition because women play critical roles in the food system, in the production, processing, preparation, consumption and distribution of food, as well as in its distribution (FAO, 2011). Yet women face discrimination and often have limited bargaining power in these roles, and the discrimination is reinforced when gender inequality intersects with other inequalities. Gender relations within the household and wider society shape the distribution of and access to food for consumption. Gender inequality shapes access to land and other resources needed to produce food, as well as the allocation of household incomes to food and other determinants of food security, such as health. Gender relations also shape the consequences of changing market conditions for both food production and distribution.

Approaching the food security challenge as a matter of imbalances between production and population obscures the complex gendered dynamics of local and global food markets, intra-household allocation of food and the production systems that are the root causes of hunger and malnutrition. Sustainable food security cannot be achieved without the agency and decision-making of women in the food system and without recognizing and overcoming the constraints that they face as producers and consumers. The policy challenge is to assess the productionist approach to food security and to reintroduce the human rights and gender perspective that privileges access, as an important component of sustainable

A policy agenda on food security must be based on an analysis of the constraints to the acquisition of food of adequate quality and quantity development. To reintroduce that perspective, the chapter highlights the structural factors at multiple levels, from the household to the global, including gender power relations and the impact of climate change, that drive food insecurity. It draws attention to the policies that are needed to address these constraints as priorities for ending hunger.

B/ FOOD INSECURITY: RECENT TRENDS

1. Persistence of hunger and malnutrition

Goal 1 of the Millennium Development Goals, and specifically the target of halving the global incidence of hunger by 2015, has been considered relatively unambitious. Monitoring progress on this goal indicates a steady decline between 1990-1992 and 2011-2013, with the proportion of people who are undernourished declining from 18.9 per cent to 12 per cent. This leaves an estimated 842 million people, or 1 in 8, undernourished[28] (FAO, 2013c). However, this understates the severity of hunger and malnutrition. According to the United Nations Children's Fund (UNICEF), 26 per cent of children, or 1 in 4, are stunted, which is evidence of long-term undernutrition that compromises the mental and physical development of the child.[29] It is estimated that 2 billion people suffer from micronutrient deficiencies, such as deficiencies of vitamin A, zinc and iron (Von Grebmer and others, 2013). Anaemia, caused by poor nutrition and deficiencies of iron and other micronutrients, affects 42 per cent of all pregnant women in the world and contributes to maternal mortality and low birth weight (World Health Organization (WHO), 2008; UNICEF, 2008).

The aggregate data on caloric undernourishment reflect nutritional outcomes averaged out over a year, and they therefore miss the uneven progress across regions and countries, and particularly at the sub-national level. Survey data on food security assessments reveal a clearer picture of the difficulties households face in meeting their food needs. The surveys find significant levels of food insecurity worldwide, even in countries with relatively low levels of food insecurity as measured by aggregate food supply. For example, the 2012 household food security survey in the United States found that 14.5 per cent of all households (17.6 million households) reported being food insecure and experienced difficulty providing enough food for all their members, and 7 million of the 17.6 million households had very low food security (Coleman-Jensen, Nord and Singh, 2013). Households with children headed by a single woman accounted for 35.4 per cent of all food-insecure households, while households headed by a single man accounted for 23.6 per cent. Women of colour, in particular, were shown to be at an extreme disadvantage (Coleman-Jensen, Nord and Singh, 2013). In South Africa, the 2012 household survey found 22 per cent of households (26% of the population) were experiencing inadequate access to food (Statistics South Africa, 2013). This contrasts sharply with the indicator used by FAO regarding the prevalence of undernutrition, which showed a very small proportion of the South African population (under 5 per cent) to be in this category during the period 2010-2012 (FAO, 2013a).

Moreover, a new form of malnutrition has emerged as an urgent challenge affecting countries in all regions of the world: obesity. Obesity as a form of malnutrition often coexists with undernutrition and results from shifts from local and traditional diets to diets that are increasingly heavy in salts, sugars and fats, characteristic of processed foods. Obesity raises the risk of cardiovascular diseases and many cancers. The global prevalence of combined overweight and obesity has risen in all regions, with the prevalence among adults increasing from 24 per cent to 34 per cent for adults between 1980 and 2008. The prevalence of obesity among children has increased even faster, doubling from 6 per cent to 12 per cent over the same period (FAO, 2013b). Overweight can co-occur with underweight within the same household, and is on the rise in countries with a high level of undernutrition, such as India and the Philippines (FAO, 2006).

2. Identifying the food insecure

Food insecurity is concentrated in South Asia and sub-Saharan Africa. Together, the two regions account for some 60 per cent of the world's undernourished (FAO, 2013a) and three quarters of stunted children (UNICEF, 2013). While progress has been significant in South Asia, it has been slower in sub-Saharan Africa, where the total number of undernourished people has only recently begun to decline.

However, the countries where food insecurity is of serious concern are not limited to these regions. Several countries in Latin America and the Caribbean (e.g., Guatemala, Haiti), South-East Asia (e.g., Cambodia, Lao People's Democratic Republic, Timor-Leste), and Central Asia (e.g., Tajikistan) figure among the 56 countries classified as having "serious", "alarming" or "very alarming" situations in the 2013 Global Hunger Index (International Food Policy Research Institute, 2013), a composite

measure that incorporates undernourishment, child underweight and child mortality. In Guatemala, the prevalence of undernourishment in the population nearly doubled from 16.2 per cent to 30.4 per cent between 1990-1992 and 2010-2012 (FAO, 2013a). In addition, the rate of malnutrition among indigenous children under 5 years old is almost double that among non-indigenous children (65.9% compared to 36.2%) (UNICEF and Central Institute for Fiscal Studies, 2011). While surveys in India show the proportion of undernourished children falling by a third, from 26 per cent to 17 per cent over the same period, more detailed data show the stubborn persistence of stunting and other forms of under-nutrition, underweight and anaemia among men and women, affecting between a quarter and over half of the population (FAO, 2013a). The limitations of national and global data sets mean that there is very little information on the gender dimensions of hunger (see box II).

The hungry are located predominantly in rural areas, where an estimated 80 per cent of the world's hungry live, among whom are smallholders (50%), landless labourers (20%) and those who depend on herding, fishing and forest resources (10%) (UNDP, 2005). The perversity of food producers and their children going hungry is captured in the case of women farm workers and their children in South Africa's commercial agricultural plantations, who experience widespread food insecurity. Faced with spiralling input prices, commercial farmers have tried "relentlessly to save on labour costs" by casualizing the labour force; this has produced devastating consequences for women farm workers both in terms of the availability of paid work and the low wages they receive.[30] Elsewhere, too, women are disproportionately affected by food insecurity. More than one third of adult women in Bangladesh, India and Pakistan are underweight (Von Grebmer and others, 2013). Hunger overlaps with other forms of vulnerability and exclusion. In India it is concentrated among women who are from low castes and scheduled tribes, from the bottom two wealth quintiles and among those who live in rural areas (Gillespie, Harris and Kadiyala, 2012; FAO, 2011).

_____

Data on food security: a key obstacle

Data gaps pose a major obstacle to gender analysis and for the monitoring of implementation of the right to food. In the most commonly used and collected international data series, for example, the proportion of undernourished or underweight children under 5 years old, there are virtually no data disaggregated by sex. Sex-disaggregated data are only collected at the national level on a limited number of internationally comparable indicators, such as body mass weight and certain micronutrient deficiencies.

The Food and Agriculture Organization of the United Nations (FAO) has developed an extensive indicator set covering multiple determinants of food security (availability, economic access, physical access, utilization, vulnerability) and outcomes (access, utilization) (FAO, 2013a). However, only 1 of the 40 indicators could be considered a gender indicator: anaemia among pregnant women. In order to assess women's realization of the right to food, it will be important to include the factors that determine their food security, disaggregated by sex, such as women's access to land and other resources, time-use and decision-making capacity.

In addition, economic data on food prices and markets are well developed for global aggregates: monthly prices on world markets for maize, rice, sugar and other commodities are monitored and published. This is valuable in understanding the overall market environment. However, more disaggregated information is needed in areas that are much less consistently monitored, but that are essential for monitoring people's access to food, including on prices at the national and local levels, and on the relationship between incomes and prices.

C/ STRUCTURAL CONSTRAINTS AND DETERMINANTS OF FOOD SECURITY

1. The paradox of plenty

For most of the twentieth century, hunger was seen as a problem of supply shortages at the national and global levels. For example, the World Food Conference, held in 1974, defined food security as: "Availability at all times of adequate world food supplies of basic foodstuffs to sustain a steady expansion of food consumption and to offset fluctuations in production and prices" (United Nations, 1975).

However, as hunger persisted, even as global production increased and food prices fell from the 1970s to the 1990s, this view of food security was challenged by many food security and policy experts (Hoddinott, 1999; Longhurst, 1988; Sen, 1982). Hunger thus came to be understood increasingly as a problem of distribution and access, and not only one of production and supply. The entitlement approach to hunger and famines developed by Amartya Sen (Sen, 1982; Drèze and Sen, 1991), and those yielded by international human rights norms, provided an intellectual and ethical foundation for the human-rights based approach to food security. Sen argued that famines occur even when there is plentiful supply, because individuals and households lose the means to acquire food (entitlements). Three means of access or entitlement were identified: wage exchange, own production, and social transfers, which would also apply in situations of endemic, or deeply-rooted and persistent, hunger and undernutrition (Drèze and Sen, 1991).

The capability to be well nourished depends not only on access to food and its utilization, but also on other capabilities such as being healthy, knowledgeable, having a say in household decision-making, and many others. Hunger and undernutrition depend on a host of economic, social and political factors that affect a person's ability to consume and utilize food that is adequate in quantity and quality. Stability of access is the other crucial component (Drèze and Sen, 1991).

Household incomes, national incomes and economic growth are important drivers of food security. Food comprises around half or more of household expenditures for low-income households under the poverty line. Abundant production drives down prices for both domestic and imported supplies. But these links are not automatic: in a paradox of plenty, hunger and malnutrition persist in contexts of plentiful and growing production and incomes. Three trends illustrate this paradox.

First, food production has more than kept pace with population growth in all regions[31] and food availability per person has improved across the world over the past two decades. At the country level, the adequacy of food supply is strongly correlated with the prevalence of undernourishment since the latter is an estimate modelled on caloric supply. However, supply is not related to other nutritional indicators, including stunting (FAO, 2013c). Countries with adequate dietary energy supply can have high levels of stunting, such as Bangladesh, Ghana and Nepal. Such persistence of malnutrition is often attributed to the ineffective utilization of food that is consumed. But it could also reflect unequal distribution of available food within the country and within the household.

Second, hunger and malnutrition persist and the latter is on the rise, in the form of obesity, in rich countries such as the United States, as well as in upper-middle-income countries such as South Africa. The rise in malnutrition reveals gaps in households' ability to access food given the prevailing distribution of income, price levels, social transfers and the physical availability of nutritious food, the supply of which is increasingly driven by the global food industries and supermarket chains. Diets are changing as people rely increasingly on purchased processed foods in place of traditional diets richer in fibre, minerals and vitamins. Middle-income countries such as Ghana, Guatemala, Namibia and others have experienced some of the most serious problems of hunger. The situation has deteriorated in Guatemala for example, where the Global Hunger Index score is worse in 2013 than it was in 1990 (IFPRI, 2013).

Third, although in developing countries household incomes are a primary means of food access, the decline in undernourishment since 1990 (9 percentage points, from 24% to 15%) has not kept pace with the decline in the incidence of income poverty (23 percentage points, from 47% to 24%). Moreover, cross-country analyses show higher levels of poverty linked to higher prevalence of under-nourishment, but with wide variance. The disconnect between income levels and hunger is more marked when considering stunting and micronutrient deficiencies. For example, Ghana has made rapid progress in reducing the incidence of household income poverty and of caloric undernourishment.But malnutrition persists, with a prevalence of stunting that still affected nearly a quarter of children who were under 5 in 2011, though this was an improvement from one third of children under 5 being affected in 1994 (FAO, 2013c).

The persistence of malnutrition in spite of improvements in household incomes is often attributed to poor utilization of food, owing to underlying health status and environmental conditions, such as a lack of access to clean water and sanitation (FAO, 2013c). But a gender analysis of structural constraints might reveal other reasons as well, notably the mal-distribution of nutritionally adequate food within households (Drèze and Sen, 1991; Harriss, 1995).

2. Food security and gender equality

(a) Gender equality, rights and capabilities

Embedded in the right to food and the entitlement approach are the principles of agency and equality. Just as the entitlement approach focuses on hunger being caused by the loss of a person's means to acquire food, the right to food "is not a right to a minimum ration of calories ... or a right to be fed. It is about being guaranteed the right to feed oneself ..." (De Schutter, 2011). Inherent in the concept of human rights is the choice of the individual in meeting those nutritional needs, and their agency in doing so. A person's ability to acquire nutritious food is therefore closely related to other aspects of their capabilities and rights.

By allowing a focus on the individual, rather than on aggregates (e.g., nation, community, household), the human rights perspective accommodates a gender analysis of food security. It can open up enquiry into the intra-household dynamics of food allocation by gender and age, examining the role of women in household and community food production, in management and in decision-making.

The central role of women in food production and household food management and the important consequences of gender relations for food security have been amply documented (Agarwal, 2012). Evidence from studies over the decades clearly shows that women face unequal constraints as producers in being able to access productive assets such as land, common property resources, machinery and livestock, credit and other financial services and improved inputs (Agarwal, 2012; FAO, 2011). The "structures of constraint" (Folbre, 1994) and inequalities that hamper women's decision-making power and control over assets and earnings result in large part from social and economic institutions, in particular: discriminatory laws, social norms, values and practices that allocate rights and responsibilities and access to resources unequally; the gender division of labour that places unequal and heavy burdens for unpaid care work and unpaid family labour within agriculture on the shoulders of women and girls; gender discrimination in labour markets that limits women's access to decent work; and unequal power relations on the basis of gender that pervade both private and public spheres and constrain the decision-making power of women and girls. As explored below, in many instances, these constraints are intensifying in the context of environmental degradation and climate change.

These systemic disadvantages that women face intersect with other forms of inequality and exclusion on the basis of low income, group identity (ethnic, racial) and location. For example, indigenous women living in rural areas are likely to be particularly disadvantaged in terms of their access to land and housing (Hernández Castillo, 2002). Likewise, low-caste women are frequently confined to the least remunerative segments of the labour market (Harriss-White and Gooptu, 2001).

Inherent in the concept of human rights is the choice of the individual in meeting their nutritional needs, and their agency in doing so

These intersecting and structural inequalities conspire to hamper women's access to adequate food, whether through own production, capacity to purchase food through earnings, or capacity to make an effective claim on social transfers (e.g., cash transfers or in-kind food provision). In addition to these three routes, the intra-household distribution of food can put girls and women in a disadvantageous position, receiving less and lower quality food than men and boys, which has been well documented for South Asia in particular (Harriss, 1995). Powerful social norms and implicit rules shape these intra-household transfers. But the problem is that when these norms and implicit rules are unfair, women are not able to claim their human rights because accountability mechanisms are not in place and there is often no redress (Elson, 2002).

(b) Rural livelihoods and gendered structures of constraint

Own production by smallholders is an important source of food security, and of livelihoods overall, in many parts of the world. Agriculture still accounts for 47 per cent of total employment in South Asia (2010-2012), and exceeds 50 per cent in most of the sub-Saharan African countries for which relevant labour force data are available, though the sector contributes much less to GDP (18% in South Asia and 14% in sub-Saharan Africa) (World Bank, 2014).

Unlike the classic transitions from agriculture to manufacturing (and from thereon to services) that took place in high-income industrialized countries, under current globalized conditions, the manufacturing sector in developing countries is unable to absorb the labour force that is being pushed out of agriculture (UNRISD, 2010; Li, 2011). At the same time, smallholder agriculture is increasingly under pressure as a viable livelihood, leading to high levels of rural poverty and outmigration. In the context of environmental degradation, it is often the men who migrate in times of difficulty and the women who are left to labour on increasingly unproductive land, while being responsible for household and family welfare (Skinner, 2011). Alongside environmental drivers, another factor in this process, as noted below, has been the shift in the policy environment, where liberalization policies have led to the withdrawal of public investment and support to agriculture.

Women farmers face both long-standing and new constraints in achieving food security. Many are systemic in nature and relate to the withdrawal of state support, in the 1980s and 1990s, for access to improved technology, credit, inputs and markets. Other constraints are anchored in social structures and power relations, including insecure rights to land, weak bargaining positions within the household and unequal access to resources and markets (FAO, International Fund for Agricultural Development and International Labour Office, 2010). In developing countries, most farmers operate or work on small farms, often in marginal environments, and/or as landless labourers. The historical institutionalized constraints to women's land ownership, through inheritance, purchase or in land reform programmes, are well documented and continue (Jacobs, 2010). While there are no global data sets to show gender inequalities in access to and ownership of land, available data show substantial gaps in diverse parts of the world: in Nepal, women own land in only 14 per cent of landowning rural households; in China, 70 per cent of farm operators without their own land are women; in Kenya, only 5 per cent of registered landowners are women; in Bangladesh and Pakistan, the land holdings of male-headed households are more than twice the size of the holdings of female-headed households (Agarwal, 2012).

Recent survey research from three diverse regional contexts provides asset data at the individual level for Ecuador, Ghana and Karnataka (India) to illustrate the scale of the problem of gender inequalities in land ownership. In Ecuador, women constitute 52 per cent of the landowners, at the national

Climate change is having
gender-differentiated impacts,
and in many cases is intensifying the
constraints that already place women
who are reliant on agriculture for
their livelihoods at a disadvantage

level; in Ghana, they represent 36 per cent of landowners; and in the state of Karnataka, India, they make up only 20 per cent (Doss and others, 2011). The differences across these contexts illustrate the strong impact of marital and inheritance regimes on women's land ownership. Ecuador has a "partial community property" marital regime, which means that all property, except for inheritances, acquired by either spouse during the marriage belongs to both of them jointly. Both Ghana and Karnataka, India, have "separation of property" marital regimes, where assets acquired during marriage belong solely to the person who purchased them. In Ecuador, children of both sexes inherit land, while there is a strong male bias in inheritance in both Ghana and India. Furthermore, survey evidence from the same three contexts suggests an association between women's land ownership and their degree of participation in agricultural decision-making (what to cultivate, how much to sell, inputs to use, etc.) (Deere and others, 2013). Women are thus likely to have greater control over what they produce and whether they use it to meet their households' food needs when they own the land.

The proportion of women in the agricultural workforce has been growing over recent decades in all regions, except in Europe, and has reached 43 per cent in Asia (which is most likely attributable to the fact that men, more than women, are exiting agriculture and seeking work in other sectors). Women rely

on agriculture more than men; of the total workforce in 2008, 57 per cent of women in Asia and 63 per cent in Africa were in work related to agriculture (Agarwal, 2012). More specifically in terms of food production, time-use surveys for parts of sub-Saharan Africa, India and China suggest that women contribute a significant proportion of the labour required to bring food to the table, if the time spent on food production, processing and preparation is aggregated (Doss, 2011). Most women, however, engage in subsistence farming, and are "trapped in low productivity cycles" (Agarwal, 2014).

Women play an important role as agricultural producers, and their work has a positive impact on national agricultural productivity. The received notion that "women produce 60-80 per cent of the world's food" may resonate with many people, but it cannot be empirically verified (Doss, 2011). But perhaps the statistical claim "obscures the complex underlying reality which is that women's labour in agriculture cannot be neatly separated from their other time uses; neither can it be separated from men's labour; nor can women's labour in agriculture be understood properly without also understanding the differential access to land, capital, assets, human capital and other productive resources" (Doss, 2011). Better data are needed, not only to understand women farmers' contributions to food production, which by all accounts is significant, but also the myriad constraints that they face, in order to formulate policies to directly address such constraints.

Climate change is having gender-differentiated impacts, and in many cases is intensifying the constraints that already place women who are reliant on agriculture for their livelihoods at a disadvantage. Women's insecure tenure rights mean they are sometimes forced to work on less productive land and are excluded from agricultural training. Less predictable rainfall, more frequent floods and droughts and more crop failures mean that greater investments are needed in technology or fertilizers, resources to which women have less access than men. Agricultural extension services have become even more important for helping farmers adapt to climate change and develop more climate-resilient practices, but they have a poor track record of reaching women. As agricultural work becomes more labour-intensive, the burden of additional work falls to women, in many cases. Climate-related health risks further add to women's unpaid work, as the main carers for their families. This has an impact on women's health and well-being and reduces the time they are able to devote to other income-generating activities. With fewer assets to fall back on and limited access to alternative sources of income, the impacts of climate change on the most food-insecure populations, and on women in particular, are overwhelmingly negative, making it more difficult to escape the traps of low-productivity work, poverty and food insecurity (Skinner, 2011).

For both female members of farming households and landless labourers in rural, peri-urban and urban areas, the right to food is largely dependent on the adequacy of their wages, which Sen (1982) refers to as "exchange entitlements". Rural labour markets are strongly gender-segregated and women are more likely than men to be working in sectors that are low-paid and do not provide adequate social protection measures. Women's entry into paid work in such contexts is sometimes driven by distress associated with rising levels of debt or the loss of earnings by other household members (FAO, 2011). Even in relatively new sectors, such as horticultural production for export, in several countries, including Chile and Mexico in Latin America and Kenya and Uganda in sub-Saharan Africa, women make up a disproportionate share of the low-paid casual and temporary workers (Barrientos and Evers, 2014).

While women's earnings can make a critical difference in pulling their households out of poverty, the adverse conditions that characterize informal rural labour markets do not bode well for women's capacity to exchange their wages and earnings for a decent standard of living, including an adequate and sustainable

supply of food. There are also gender-specific constraints on women's ability to control and decide how their earnings are spent (Kabeer, 2007). Efforts to regulate the wages and earnings of low-paid and informal workers are critical if this exchange entitlement is to function. This is not always easy, given the limited reach of local trade unions in rural areas. In Uganda, however, women flower workers have campaigned successfully, with the support of an international non-governmental organization, Women Working Worldwide, for higher overtime pay, better working hours and freedom of association, even if their real wages remained low as a result of high inflation rates in 2010-2011 (Barrientos and Evers, 2014).

A related issue from a gender perspective is the intra-household distribution of food. This may not be susceptible to policy influence, but easing pressures on food-insecure households, whether through general income support, food subsidies or school feeding programmes, can reduce the negative impact of intra-household gender bias in the distribution of food. Conversely, when households cannot access sufficient food, this bias is likely to be reinforced, with dire consequences for the health and nutritional status of women and girls. Hence, in the context of current food price hikes, cuts to food subsidies as part of austerity programmes undertaken in many developing countries are of serious concern (Hossain, King and Kelbert, 2013; UN-Women, 2014). A broader agenda for government and civil society is to promote the awareness of women's and girls' right to food and to empower them to claim that right by confronting gender bias and discrimination in the intra-household allocation of food.

The historically entrenched constraints outlined above, combined with new challenges driven by transformations of the food system and markets, as discussed in the next section, affect food-insecure people and households in a variety of contexts as consumers and producers. However, they have a particularly negative impact on smallholders who, as already noted, are also the largest group among food-insecure populations.

D/ EMERGING CHALLENGES: THE GLOBAL FOOD SYSTEM

The food production and distribution systems of the twenty-first century are markedly different from those of the previous century and pose new threats to food security, particularly for poor households in poor countries, often with gendered consequences (High-level Panel of Experts on Food Security and Nutrition, 2011; von Braun, 2014).

The first reason for this change is that the global market has dramatically shifted. While the 1970s, 1980s and 1990s were characterized by abundant production and low international food prices, the current context is marked by rising and volatile world market prices and constraints to production. Development aid for agriculture plummeted during the 1980s and through the 1990s until the 2000s. Simultaneously, the governments of developing countries were advised by the international financial institutions to reduce the scope of state investment in agriculture and in agricultural research. This has been associated with low yields, especially in tropical agriculture, and the falling productivity of land. At the same time, greater trade openness and increasing market orientation of farmers have encouraged a shift away from food crops that were better suited to local ecological and social conditions, to cash crops, which require the purchase of inputs. With the cutback in public funding of agricultural inputs, farmers, especially women farmers, have been left at the mercy of large seed and fertilizer companies, marketing agents and moneylenders (Ghosh, 2010). These factors have contributed to the prolonged agrarian crisis in many developing countries.

After decades of low prices since the 1970s, world food prices began to rise from the early 2000s and peaked sharply over the period 2007-2008. Though domestic prices do not always mirror international price trends and levels, the 2007-2008 price hikes led to sharp rises in food prices in most developing countries (High-level Panel of Experts on Food Security and Nutrition, 2011). World market price increases therefore threaten food security for poor households. For example, the 2011 increase in the price of basic grains meant that, in many developing countries, the cost of a kilogram of wheat doubled from about $0.15 to $0.30, a critical difference for people who live on little more than a dollar a day (von Braun, 2014). Food represents a substantial portion of the expenditure of poor households in poor countries. For countries in Asia and Africa with available data, expenditure on food was generally over 50 per cent in the early 2000s, prior to the 2007-2008 crisis (e.g., 76% in Kenya, 75% in Pakistan, 63% in the Philippines) compared with a range of expenditure on food of between 10 per cent and 25 per cent in Western Europe and North America (e.g., 24% in France, 18% in the United States, 11% in the Netherlands) (FAO, 2013a).

While in theory, higher prices can increase incomes and stimulate production, in reality, when farmers lack the necessary inputs and resources, they are less able to respond to such price incentives. Moreover, higher prices do not neatly trickle down to the farm gate. Households adjust to such a decline in their capacity to purchase food in a variety of ways, including by shifting to less costly and less diverse diets, which are often deficient in the essential nutrients that are particularly important for pregnant women and young children. Studies of 11 countries with data available found that, in 8 of those countries, malnutrition increased or improvements in nutrition slowed during the period from 2007 to 2010 (von Braun,

2014). Women bear the brunt of coping with food insecurity, often by reducing their own consumption in favour of other members of the household and by spending more time on food preparation and processing, thereby adding to their unpaid care work (Quisumbing and others, 2008). FAO estimates that some 173 million individuals were added to the number of undernourished people between 2007 and 2009 (High-level Panel of Experts on Food Security and Nutrition, 2011).

The second factor to be taken into consideration is that climate change is likely to drive shifts in production potential throughout the world, thereby affecting productivity and prices. Studies consistently point to overwhelmingly negative consequences for farmers in the most vulnerable environments (Nelson and others, 2009). As the High-level Panel of Experts on Food Security and Nutrition (2012) noted, vulnerability to food insecurity arises both from biophysical and socioeconomic factors: "pre-existing conditions of vulnerability make poor people more exposed to the effects of climate change, as social, economic and agroenvironmental circumstances may become more severe with climate change". Since 1975, disasters have claimed the lives of more than 2.2 million people, with climate-related storms, floods, droughts, heat waves and other weather-related phenomena responsible for two thirds of the fatalities and economic losses resulting from disasters (United Nations, International Strategy for Disaster Reduction (secretariat), 2009).

Rising temperatures, changing precipitation patterns and extreme weather events will increase the likelihood of crop failures, reduce yields and encourage pests and weeds. Scenario studies by the International Food Policy Research Institute predict major yield and production losses for wheat, rice and maize in the most food-insecure regions: South Asia and sub-Saharan Africa (Nelson and others, 2009). Dryland agriculture in arid and semi-arid regions, where over 40 per cent of the world's population and more than 650 million of the poorest and most food-insecure people live, is especially vulnerable to the risks of climate change and variability, drought in particular. In some regions of the world, significant agricultural production takes place in low-lying coastal areas, where current population densities are high. In these regions, and particularly in small island States, a major threat of climate change is from saline intrusion, sea-level rise and increased flooding (High-level Panel of Experts on Food Security and Nutrition, 2012). Assuming no climate adaptation investments are made, child malnutrition could increase by 20 per cent by 2050, which would erase the gains made in previous decades (Nelson and others, 2009). The consequences are likely to be particularly severe for women smallholders, who are the least equipped to adapt to changing conditions, in large part because of the constraints they face in accessing such resources as credit, information and inputs that facilitate adaptive production strategies (Agarwal, 2012; Quisumbing and others, 2008).

The context of climate change and demands for mitigation of emissions in high-income countries has also led to the rise of the biofuel industry. Biofuel production has grown dramatically since the early 2000s. For example, between 2000-2002 and 2007-2009, ethanol production increased more than five-fold in the United

Women bear the brunt of coping with food insecurity, often by reducing their own consumption in favour of other members of the household and by spending more time on food preparation and processing, thereby adding to their unpaid care work

States and in the European Union, and it more than doubled in Brazil. While the European Union, the United States, Brazil, China and India are the largest consumers of biofuels, production is dominated by the United States and Brazil, which together account for 75 per cent of the global ethanol supply, while the European Union produces almost 80 per cent of biodiesel generated from canola. The High-level Panel of Experts on Food Security and Nutrition (2011) explains that this development was "made possible only because of massive public support: subsidies, tax exemption and mandatory use in gasoline [which] in 2009 ... reached about 8 billion dollars in the European Union and the United States ... at the same time as they have reduced support for agricultural production, both at home and in their overseas assistance to poor countries".

A third factor in bringing about the change is that food as a globally traded commodity has become integrated into a more complex financial market, closely related not only to fuel but interlinked with other forces in the financial market. The price spikes of 2007-2008 were related to the fuel and financial crises of 2008. While they were not the sole factor driving prices, and shifts in demand and supply explain much of the upward pressure on world market prices, many argue that speculative activities are likely to have played a role in driving the spikes for some commodities (Ghosh, 2010; High-level Panel of Experts on Food Security and Nutrition, 2011).

A fourth aspect in this scenario concerns the domestic and international economic policy environments, which have shifted, but in unbalanced ways. Producers around the world benefited from domestic state support in the twentieth century through a variety of policy interventions, public investments and price support and stabilization measures, including the holding of reserve stocks (De Schutter, 2011). Most developing countries removed these interventions during the 1980s and 1990s, as a part of liberalization and structural adjustment measures. However, the shifts in agricultural

policy were less radical in OECD countries, which maintained their support structures to farmers. Export subsidies and farm income support, which benefit farmers in the developed world, depress prices in world markets and create unfair competition for poor farmers and poor countries. The results of these market pressures can have particularly harsh consequences for food security.

The Agreement Establishing the World Trade Organization, of 1994, and a series of multilateral trade agreements, had major consequences for domestic agricultural support policies. Restrictions on trade-distorting domestic support measures in the Agreement on Agriculture have been controversial. Developing countries have consistently contested the provisions, arguing that the measures conflict with the objectives of food security and poverty reduction (De Schutter, 2011). The issue was highlighted once more at the Ninth Ministerial Conference of the World Trade Organization, held in Bali, Indonesia, in 2013, where 33 developing countries with significant smallholder populations tabled a proposal on reforming the provisions regarding the ability of governments to purchase food from domestic producers at reasonable prices for public stocks.

The fifth element that has brought about change, stimulated by increasing volatility and rising prices in world food markets, is investment in agricultural land, often referred to as "land grabs", which has been growing rapidly since the 2006-2008 food and commodity price boom (Borras and others, 2011; GRAIN, 2008). Investors include foreign financial entities, such as hedge funds and pension funds diversifying their portfolios, but also governments aiming to secure food supplies for their populations. Such investments have been an important factor behind the expansion of cultivated land, which has totalled about 5.5 million hectares per year in developing countries over the period from 1990 to 2007 (Deininger and Byerlee, 2011). They are making it difficult for poor and marginalized farmers, as well as pastoralists, to maintain their access to land, in many cases resulting in their dispossession. Such farmers, particularly women, tend to have insecure rights to land, which their families may have cultivated for generations, owing to lack of registration or ambiguities about the nature of land rights that are often interpreted as limited to usufruct (FAO, International Fund for Agricultural Development and International Labour Office, 2010). Large-scale investments in agricultural land might have positive benefits for aggregate GDP growth, national food production and employment creation. They could also open up new markets and technologies for the agricultural sector that would have spillover effects on smallholders (Deininger and Byerlee, 2011). Yet it is clear that their consequences for marginalized farmers who are dispossessed are likely to be negative. Furthermore, contemporary and historical experience provide consistent lessons regarding the negative impacts of dispossession on women: their lack of decision-making power on resettlement schemes; discriminatory compensation; exclusion from common property resources on which they are disproportionately dependent; and general deterioration in their well-being and status (see box III).

Box III
_____

Gendered effects of "land grabs"

While States have long dispossessed rural peoples of their land for development purposes, so-called "land grabbing" is now attracting unprecedented attention. Land grabs at a global level are increasing, they are changing in character, and they are generating significant political opposition. Estimates indicate that between 50 million and 66 million people were displaced from their land in China between 1980 and 2002, and some 60 million people have been displaced in India since 1947, with the rate increasing in the past two decades, accounting for the majority of the world's dispossessed persons (if not the majority of dispossessed land area). In the twentieth century, most "development-induced displacement" was as a result of large public infrastructure and industrial projects, including public sector dams, mines and heavy industries. In many countries of Africa, Latin America and South-East Asia, international agribusiness, finance capital and foreign States are acquiring large areas of agricultural land.

A study of several cases of land grabbing and dispossession worldwide revealed that rare and limited gains were overwhelmed by a confluence of exclusions and gender inequalities. The negative consequences of land dispossession in the context of development projects recur with remarkable regularity, irrespective of project type and social context. First, in none of the cases examined did women have any decision-making power in the planning of projects or in negotiating the details of resettlement and rehabilitation. Second, discriminatory compensation and resettlement almost universally reproduced women's lack of land rights, or undermined them where they actually existed, by allocating compensation land or plots to male heads of households. In addition to land, states also directed other forms of compensation, whether cash or jobs, to men, thereby undermining women's influence over its allocation. Third, as women are the most dependent on common property resources for work and income in most agrarian contexts, they are the most affected by the enclosure of land, the destruction of commons and the resulting losses of livestock. Fourth, while the causal link between land dispossession and domestic violence and alcoholism remains underspecified, the increase of both has been observed by almost all studies of displaced populations. Fifth, since dispossession entails removing people from land against their will, states often resort to violence to push projects through, creating situations in which women's physical security becomes particularly at risk. The record of development-induced displacement is replete with examples of sexual violence and other human rights abuses perpetrated by the police, the army or hired thugs. Finally, in all cases, women widely recognized the threats dispossession posed or ultimately created for their well-being and played important roles in both overt and covert opposition to land grabs.

While it is important to recognize that the consequences were also typically poor for men, overall, whether women's labour was marginalized or increasingly exploited after dispossession, in none of the cases was women's well-being and social position improved by the development projects for which they gave their land. Indeed, the level of discrimination in the gender and social relations that structure women's work within and outside the household was arguably increased.

This points to the urgent need to maintain and defend democratically determined definitions of the public good, to limit the forcible acquisition of land to that needed for public projects with widespread benefits for the poor, especially poor women, and to make prior and informed consent a prerequisite for private projects that require land. It goes without saying that such consent must be obtained by all members of affected populations (including those without formal land rights) and not simply heads of household: this would also help to ensure that only those projects from which women can expect to benefit would move forward.

Source: Levien, 2014.

E/ NATIONAL EFFORTS TO SECURE THE RIGHT TO FOOD

While acknowledging that the global context has presented disabling conditions for the realization of the right to food, the governments of developing countries do have policy options. For national governments, giving priority to human rights can involve difficult choices when policies to promote food security potentially conflict with macroeconomic objectives and international trade rules (De Schutter, 2011). There is broad agreement among the food and nutrition policy community on a number of core policy priorities for promoting food security as a public good: (a) reversing the under-investment in agriculture and support to smallholders, for example, through research and development, investment in climate-resilient agriculture,

Extension services need to be overhauled in order to integrate the specific concerns of women farmers in the context of climate change and to facilitate the exchange of knowledge and good practices

access to irrigation, affordable institutional credit and extension services and making sure that they reach women farmers; (b) removing gender discrimination in access to land and agricultural services; (c) robust social protection measures to increase the purchasing power of households; and (d) social investments to improve health and education, especially of women, and thereby improve nutrition. Measures that involve greater government intervention are increasingly being adopted by many developing countries, as outlined below.

There is now widespread agreement on the need for governments to invest in climate-resilient agriculture. The High-level Panel of Experts on Food Security and Nutrition makes the case that policies at the national level to increase general food system resilience are very likely to contribute to climate adaptation also, concluding that increases in expenditure on adaptation would be better directed at increasing overall expenditure on sustainable food security, with particular attention to the particular challenges posed by climate change. Such approaches will be very specific to particular locations and should draw on the knowledge of farmers, including women smallholders. As the High-level Panel of Experts (2011) has noted, "there will be no environmentally sustainable agriculture without the involvement and initiative of smallholders".

Extension services, which have often failed to effectively target women, need to be overhauled in order to integrate the specific concerns of

women farmers in the context of climate change and to facilitate the exchange of knowledge and good practices. Governments should also seize the opportunity to address the barriers to women's access to financial services, such as credit and microinsurance, in order to enable them to make the changes to farming practices that are needed to secure their access to food, as the environmental context changes (High-level Panel of Experts on Food Security and Nutrition, 2012). Good practices at the community level include improved water management, such as building more efficient systems for irrigation

This farmer is part of a regional cassava
initiative that supports vulnerable
smallholders in eastern and central Africa

and water capture, storage and use; adopting practices to conserve soil moisture, organic matter and nutrients; and setting up community-based seed and grain banks. In Malawi, for example, women smallholders in several communities have developed strategies to overcome acute food shortages by using ecological cropping techniques that enable them to take advantage of changing rainfall periods in order to produce a second maize crop (Skinner, 2011).

Mobilizing women's agency and knowledge will be needed in attempts to foster sustainable and climate-resilient agricultural practices. Women Organizing for Change in Agriculture and Natural Resource Management, a global network of professionals and farmers across 83 countries, provides an important example of how this can be done. The network is dedicated to increasing women's access to and control of resources and integrating gender into agricultural policies. It works at the community level, but also works to make national policies, programmes and institutions more responsive to the needs and potential of rural women and to integrate them more effectively into the design, implementation and monitoring of policies. Forums of this nature are important, since research shows that any easy assumptions regarding the interests of women farmers aligning perfectly with policies on environmentally sustainable agriculture, at the local and national levels, can be misplaced (Agarwal, 2014). Women's participation in deliberating policy options is therefore critical.

Such measures as price supports and input subsidies for production and income stabilization, price controls on essential food items to limit household expenditures on food, and public food stocks to moderate price volatility, were commonly used in developing countries, but were discontinued under agricultural liberalization programmes since the 1980s. However, they have recently been reconsidered in a number of countries and redesigned as policy tools for reducing hunger and food insecurity. Many of these experiences have had positive results.

For example, input subsidies on fertilizers and seeds were largely dismantled during the 1980s as part of the structural adjustment reforms in developing countries. Critics of subsidies argue that they distort prices and often have perverse distributional effects, benefiting well-off producers and agribusinesses. However, newer debates have led to a reverse trend, starting in the late 1990s, to develop "smart" subsidies that are more targeted and could have broader social and economic benefits (Tiba, 2011). Ghana, Kenya, Malawi, Mali, Nigeria, Rwanda, Senegal and the United Republic of Tanzania, among other countries, have recently introduced new input subsidy programmes.

Another policy approach that is gaining ground is public procurement from smallholders. This addresses the institutional constraints they face, particularly rife in the case of women farmers, in accessing markets and obtaining fair prices, while providing a better quality of food products to social programmes, such as schools, hospitals and canteens, and helping to diversify diets with fresh produce. It is a key aspect of India's new food security policy, launched in 2013. Brazil

has made extensive use of this approach as a major element of the country's comprehensive food security policy, *Fome Zero* (Zero Hunger), implemented since 2003, which has contributed to the sustained decline in hunger in rural areas, especially among female-headed households. The programme is being replicated in several countries in sub-Saharan Africa.

Public food reserves were one of the major food security policies throughout the twentieth century, but were largely dismantled in the 1980s in the context of structural adjustment reforms. Critics argue that they are inefficient and ineffective, expensive and complex to manage, and that they distort incentives for private storage that can more effectively offset supply fluctuations. However, it is also acknowledged that food stocks have been effective in stabilizing prices, as well as in stimulating agricultural growth (FAO, 2011; Crola, 2011). Many rice-producing countries in Asia have long used buffer stocks, as well as export and import monopolies and public procurement as complementary tools for price stabilization. More recently, Burkina Faso, Indonesia and Madagascar have implemented effective stock programmes (Crola, 2011). Moreover, proposals are being discussed for international food reserves as a mechanism to reduce the risks of price hikes in world food markets (Wright, 2012).

The other mechanism for guaranteeing the right to adequate food is through social transfers (e.g., in-kind transfers such as through direct public provision of subsidized food). Smallholders and landless agricultural labourers are particularly susceptible to the socioeconomic effects of climate change, especially if increased climate variability is not accompanied by improved social protection measures. Many governments provide subsidies on food to both rural and urban populations in order to enhance food security. The concern about food wastage and "leakage" of subsidies to the non-poor has led to a reconsideration of such programmes, and sometimes to arguments for replacing them with cash transfers. While cash transfers may be administratively easier to handle, the drawback is that the purchasing power of such cash transfers can be eroded in the context of food price rises. A further concern from a gender perspective is that cash transfers can be spent on other household priorities or needs and such items as alcohol and tobacco. In order to ensure the food security of girls and women in particular, the direct provision of affordable food may thus be the better option, a position that was strongly endorsed in a survey with women slum dwellers in New Delhi (Ghosh, 2011).

The experience of Brazil is instructive in this regard. The policy instruments discussed, including public procurement, food stocks and price supports, are elements of *Fome Zero* that bolster each of the entitlements (production, exchange and transfers) through which households can acquire food. The programme also supports access to credit, inputs and other resources for smallholders, cash transfers (*Bolsa Familia*, a programme which is largely directed at women), public procurement from family farms, increases in social investments and a minimum wage that has more than doubled since 2003. Food security is a consistent priority across different social and economic policies, including Brazil's trade policies and positions in multilateral policy forums.

The Agreement on Agriculture addresses national support measures for agriculture and sets minimum allowable levels of trade-distorting measures, evaluated by a complex set of criteria. Overall, these provisions leave much broader policy scope for developed countries than for developing countries. The level of support to agriculture in developed countries remains very high, based on a wide range of government subsidies that are not considered trade-distorting and are therefore permitted (Demeke and others, 2012). For developing countries, there are more constraints in the formulation of a robust set of food security policies, in part because the Agreement on Agriculture was designed in the 1980s and 1990s, when developing countries were being encouraged to liberalize the sector in order to stimulate production. Food security in poor countries and households was not the major concern. Many of the support measures fall into a "grey zone" and countries face uncertainty as to the

trade consequences of adopting them and being exposed to potential litigation (De Schutter, 2011).

Apart from the overall negative effect of these measures on producers in developing countries, there are clear inconsistencies between these trade measures and the objective of ending the unacceptably high level of hunger and malnutrition. Supporting the productivity of smallholders in developing countries, notably in sub-Saharan Africa and South Asia, would help to facilitate the achievement of that objective (De Schutter, 2011). A second important point is the inequity in these global trade rules, where income support to farmers in the European Union and the United States does not face the same restrictions as subsidies to consumers in India. Trade rules accommodate measures that emerged in developed countries to suppress production in an era of depressed prices and abundant production. They need to be changed to meet the needs of the twenty-first century and the challenge of high prices and potential new pressures on production from climate change, polluting technology and competition for fuel (De Schutter, 2011).

The right to food remains an unfulfilled human right and an urgent global challenge. Food security policies should address the structural causes constraining people's access to food at the local, national and global levels. A supply-driven framework does not adequately address the structural inequalities that constrain women's and girls' access to adequate food, whether through own production, earnings/ food exchange, intra-household distribution or social transfers. A new agenda for food security in the context of sustainable development needs to refocus attention on people's capabilities and rights, on public goods and on the key issues that determine access. If sustainable development is to include gender equality at its centre, then issues of access and rights, and the structural forces that constrain access and rights from the micro to the macro level, need to be tackled head-on. If this process is to be successful, the agency, leadership and decision-making power of women will be critical.

CHAPTER /5
POPULATION, SUSTAINABLE DEVELOPMENT AND GENDER EQUALITY

A/ INTRODUCTION

Population is a crucial aspect of sustainable development across its three dimensions. Population growth and decline, urban/rural location, migration, composition in terms of sex and age and a host of other factors all have an impact on economic growth and labour markets, health, the environment and the prospects for present and future generations. Population dynamics can significantly influence the possibilities for achieving a socially just and gender-responsive approach to sustainable development. The topic of population elicits debates about the relationships between humans and nature, men and women, old and young, rich and poor. Population policies often centre on women's health, reproduction and sexuality. Population paradigms frequently attribute poverty to overpopulation; see the causes of environmental degradation and natural resource scarcity in population growth or mismanagement by poor people; and link reducing women's fertility to mitigating climate change or preventing environmental destruction (UNDP, 2011).

In an era of climate change, financial instability and growing inequalities, concerns about overpopulation play an important role. Population growth has an impact on the natural environment, human society and prospects for sustainable development. However, the dominant focus on population growth shifts attention away from unsustainable patterns and levels of production and consumption, particularly regarding the stark differences in resource distribution and levels of consumption both between and within countries, which pose significant challenges for sustainability. The relationship between population and sustainability is context-specific and mediated by a host of other factors, economic, political, social and cultural.

Critically, focusing on overpopulation as a root cause of these problems often leads to problematic policy responses, particularly from a gender perspective. Population policies that are coercive in their approach to reducing fertility rates compromise human well-being, dignity, individual bodily integrity and autonomy and are inconsistent with international norms and standards. Since 1994, the global policy and normative framework has made a significant shift in recognizing women's sexual and reproductive health and reproductive rights as the cornerstone of population and development policies. Both the Programme of Action of the International Conference on Population and Development and the Beijing Declaration and Platform for Action, and the subsequent outcomes of their review conferences, have reaffirmed the centrality of sexual and reproductive health and reproductive rights to sustainable development. The recent 20-year review process concerning the implementation of the Programme of Action of the International Conference on Population and Development highlighted the need for sustainable development policies to be grounded in human

Population policies that are coercive in their approach to reducing fertility rates compromise human well-being, dignity, individual bodily integrity and autonomy and are inconsistent with international norms and standards rights, non-discrimination, gender equality and sexual and reproductive health and rights (see A/69/62).

The achievement of sexual and reproductive health and rights for all people will necessitate a new social contract, where governments meet their obligations as duty bearers and individuals claim their rights. Sexual and reproductive health and rights include rights to access essential information, education and services for all on issues such as sexuality, relationships, pregnancies and safe childbirth. This includes recognition of the basic right of all couples and individuals to decide freely and responsibly on the number, spacing and timing of their children and to have the information and means to do so. The human rights of women include their right to have control over and decide freely and responsibly on matters related to their sexuality, including sexual and reproductive health, free of coercion, discrimination and violence. The enjoyment of sexual and reproductive health and rights includes the right of access to sexual and reproductive health-care services of high quality across the life cycle, including safe and effective family planning methods and

emergency obstetric care, recognizing the right of women and men to be informed and to have access to safe, effective, affordable and acceptable methods of family planning of their choice.[32] Among the obstacles to advancing this agenda are narratives linking population growth to environmental degradation, which pervade popular media, environmental education and policy debates and decisions in the health, conservation and climate arenas. These narratives have influenced the way current demographic dynamics are related to gender and sustainability and the design of policies.

This chapter explores the debates on overpopulation, gender equality and sustainable development and serves as a prompt to policymakers to go beyond the limits of overpopulation paradigms in order to better understand the complex interplay of contributors to global problems. This means responding to the most significant drivers of environmental challenges, including patterns and levels of unsustainable production and consumption, and firmly anchoring sustainable development policies in human rights, including sexual and reproductive health and rights.

B/ DEMOGRAPHIC DYNAMICS

1. Current population picture

Present demographic realities are very different from what they were even 50 years ago. Over the course of the twentieth century, world population almost quadrupled, from 1.65 billion in 1900 to around 6.1 billion in 2000 (United Nations, 1999; 2001). However, what was termed a "population explosion" is now slowing down. World population growth rates have

been declining since the late 1960s, with birth rates declining more rapidly than anticipated. Smaller households are becoming the global norm.

At present, the average number of children per woman, measured as the total fertility rate,[33] is estimated to be 2.53 for the period from 2005 to 2010, according to the *World Population Prospects: The 2012 Revision* (United Nations,

World population growth rates have been declining since the late 1960s, with birth rates declining more rapidly than anticipated

2013c). That figure masks differences between countries. Sub-Saharan Africa has 39 countries with a total fertility rate above 4, and among these, 10 countries: Angola, Burkina Faso, Burundi, Chad, the Democratic Republic of the Congo, Mali, the Niger, Nigeria, Somalia and Uganda, have total fertility rates above 6.[34] Nevertheless, fertility rates are declining in most of these countries, especially in urban areas. In other countries, mainly in East Asia and Eastern Europe, fertility rates have fallen well below replacement-level fertility of roughly 2 children per woman. However, the population is not yet declining in most of those countries, owing to population momentum, except in countries such as Japan that are most advanced in the demographic transition (Fischer, 2014). During the period from 2005 to 2010, the 75 countries with below-replacement fertility made up 48 per cent of the world's population (United Nations, 2013c).

The result is heterogeneity of demographic experiences around the world: "The demographic transition associated with declining fertility and mortality levels, together with the urban transition that has shifted the locus of human activity from rural to urban areas, have caused unprecedented changes in population size, age structures and spatial distribution" (A/69/62, para. 760).

The *World Population Prospects*: The *2012 Revision* estimates that the present world population of about 7.2 billion in 2014 will reach 8.1 billion in 2025, 9.6 billion in 2050 and 10.9 billion by 2100. These calculations are based on the medium-variant projection, the one most widely used. The projected global population total is higher than in the 2010 revision, which estimated a population of 10.1 billion in 2100. This is mainly because projected fertility levels have been adjusted upward in a number of countries, particularly in sub-Saharan Africa (United Nations, 2013c).

Age structure matters. A large cohort of people of reproductive age in a population generates demographic momentum, as there are more people having children than in an ageing population. Today, in developed countries as a whole, 23 per cent of the population is already aged 60 or older, surpassing the percentage of children aged 15 and under (United Nations, 2013c). While most developing countries have more youthful populations, and hence more demographic momentum, declining fertility rates mean that they too will increasingly face the phenomenon of population ageing.

The projection that the world population may grow to almost 11 billion people is being met with a call for greater investments in family planning in order to reduce population growth (United Nations, 2013c). However, a narrow focus on contraception and family planning overlooks the complex interplay of social, economic and cultural factors in demographic transitions to lower birth rates. Family planning policies should be situated within a broader sexual and reproductive health and rights and gender equality framework, rather than solely focusing on fertility reduction.

2. Population dynamics

Youthful and ageing populations are population dynamics which generate significant policy debate. Children and young people are the majority of the population in the global South, with 1.7 billion children under the age of 15 and 1.1 billion young people aged 15-24, the largest global cohort of young people in history. Youthful populations predominate in countries that are considered to be the least developed, including Mali, the Niger and Somalia, which also have the highest population growth rates (United Nations, 2013c).

The youthful population boom in the global South is expected to generate substantial social change on an international scale (A/69/62). Two theories, namely, the demographic dividend and the youth bulge, dominate scholarly and policy discussions about how youth will influence economics, politics and international security. The demographic dividend concept suggests that large youthful populations can create economic growth and development under the right conditions, including increased access to education for young people and economic policies that support open trade. Population policy would be a key tool for achieving dividends because it influences fertility rates and creates a large proportion of working age adults to dependent seniors and children.

In contrast, the youth bulge theory predicts that large youth populations are prone to violence and unrest at a variety of levels and intensities. Urdal (2012) suggests that youth bulge violence is not inevitable, but is

It is equally important to recognize the diversity of ageing populations. Population ageing, when the number of older people in the population increases and the number of young people decreases, is occurring throughout the world. It is most concentrated in the developed countries, including in Italy, Japan and the Russian Federation, where the number of older people exceeds the number of those under 15 years of age. The *World Population Prospects: The 2012 Revision* reports that by 2050 there will be close to double the number of older people than children in developed countries (United Nations, 2013c). The diminishing birth rates in developed countries, coupled with the longevity of ageing populations, are causing fears of economic stagnation on the basis of assumptions about the lack of working age adults and rising health-care costs. Ageing populations are often seen as economic drains on national economies.

The popular linkage of large "greying" populations with economic decline ignores the

Recognizing and respecting the variety of experiences and aspirations among young people is necessary to design policies that enable the realization of human rights and capabilities

attributable to a combination of population stress and lack of employment, resources and education for young people. As such, states can mitigate or harness the impact of youth bulges through providing increased educational and employment opportunities.

This binary understanding of youth populations as either a dividend or a bulge leads to policy responses that treat youth as a homogeneous group, without the recognition of diversity. Recognizing and respecting the variety of experiences and aspirations among young people is necessary to design policies that enable the realization of human rights and capabilities.

multiple roles older people play as paid and unpaid workers, including in the care economy, and as consumers and investors. The notion that ageing populations act as a drain on national economies, coupled with alarm over their size and longevity and fears of pension scarcity, have been used as a rationale for pension privatization in developed countries. Pension privatization, however, is largely driven by opportunities to open up new markets and increase the flow of capital. As Minns and Sexton (2006) conclude, "if there is a crisis of too many old people, it is one of too many people in poverty in their old age, both now and in the future. Problems of pension financing derive less from demographic changes than from unemployment, low wages, and a shift in income distribution away from wages towards profits".

Population ageing also raises urgent questions about the adequacy of existing care systems (both paid and unpaid), especially in the case of those whose meagre savings and pensions do not allow them to access market-based care services. Women are disproportionately represented among this group, given their generally higher life expectancy, their smaller savings and limited access to contributory pensions, and the fact that they are more likely to marry, or cohabit, with men who are older than they are; this means that women are more likely to provide care for their spouses but less likely to receive care from them in their old age (Abe, 2010; Arza, 2014). In the context of changes in household structures (the increasing proportion of one-person households and households that include only elderly persons, in some contexts) and, to some degree, changes in the labour market (the increase in female labour force participation), policymakers need to put in place adequate care systems, such as Japan's long-term care insurance, which has made a small but significant impact in reducing the long hours of unpaid care provided by family members, especially female spouses and daughters (Abe, 2010).

3. Demographic transitions and family planning

Demographic transition is a process whereby reductions in mortality are followed by reductions in fertility. Together, these reductions eventually lead to smaller proportions of children and larger proportionate shares of older people in the population (United Nations, 2013d). The process of demographic transition leads populations to experience a period of population growth owing to natural increase, along with the processes of urbanization and population ageing (Dyson, 2010).

While initially demographers posited that industrialization would bring about declines in mortality and fertility in developing countries, by the 1960s they began to identify rapid population growth in poor countries as a serious brake on economic development; hence, a decline in fertility came to be seen as a prerequisite for, and not a consequence of, successful industrialization (Hodgson, 1983; Szreter, 1993). As such, policy responses based on the idea that family planning could induce demographic transition emerged from the 1960s to 1990s.

The assumed link between family planning and demographic transition yielded a number of rationales for population control, including the view that investments in family planning were much more cost-effective than other development strategies (Connelly, 2008). Family planning programmes and contraception play a role as one among many proximate factors that influence the timing and speed of fertility decline. However, broader and contextual factors, including economic, social and cultural differences between countries, even in the same region, influence the shape and timing of declines in mortality and fertility, rather than family planning alone.

Mortality decline also needs to be viewed from a gender perspective. Women and girls are more likely to die than men and boys in many low- and middle-income countries than they are in rich countries, resulting in some 3.9 million excess deaths of girls and women under the age of 60.[36] Of these 3.9 million excess deaths, one fifth of girls die in infancy, two fifths of girls and women die in their reproductive years, and around two fifths are accounted for by sex-selective abortion of female foetuses (the "missing girls"), and the numbers are growing in sub-Saharan Africa and in the countries most affected by HIV/AIDS (World Bank, 2012).

The causes of maternal mortality are complex and vary by region. Between 2003 and 2009, 73 per cent of all maternal deaths were the result of direct obstetric causes (e.g., haemorrhage, hypertensive disorders, sepsis, embolism), including 8 per cent caused by complications related to unsafe abortions, and the 27 per cent were the result of indirect causes (e.g., HIV-related, pre-existing medical conditions) (Say and others, 2014). Therefore, while family planning represents one aspect of the response needed to reduce maternal mortality, a broader sexual and reproductive health and rights agenda, including access to quality sexual and reproductive health services, is necessary.

C/ POPULATION AND THE ENVIRONMENT:
POLICIES AND CONSEQUENCES

Concerns about overpopulation play a central role in the main discourses about sustainable development and policy responses. These concerns draw on older theories and models about the relationship between population, resources and the environment that have proved remarkably resilient. Among these notions are "carrying capacity", which is related to planetary boundaries, as discussed in chapter I, "the tragedy of the commons", which is concerned with the management of common resources, and degradation narratives that refer to environmental destruction by the poor.

There are a number of reasons for the resilience of concerns about overpopulation. First, even though these notions may have been disproven by historical evidence (Ostrom, 2000; Boyce, Narain and Stanton, 2007), overpopulation paradigms project population-induced scarcities into the future. Because sustainable development takes a long-term and future-oriented view, such projections are appealing: they seem to provide insight into what lies ahead for humanity.

Second, overpopulation paradigms make hunger, poverty, environmental degradation and even war seem like the inevitable consequence of too many people pressing up against too few resources. By avoiding the political negotiation of resource use and control, competition and conflict, these paradigms can shift responsibilities away from powerful elites and vested interests onto the shoulders of the poor.

Third, these paradigms draw on and reinforce dominant and stereotyped views of women and men. Women matter only to the extent that they reproduce the population problem. In some cases, women's agency is recognized, but only in a limited fashion as enlightened managers of their own fertility and local environments. Gender power relations, as well as differences between women on the basis of other factors, tend to be overlooked.

Demographic dynamics are indeed complex. The problem with the paradigms presented below is that they ignore this complexity and reduce demographic dynamics to the operation of abstract laws that can justify coercive measures and narrow policy responses. Analysing population paradigms is a necessary first step in rethinking the relationships between gender, population dynamics and the environment in order to make more effective policies.

1. Perspectives on population, sustainability and gender equality

Narratives linking population, poverty and environmental degradation gained increasing traction in policy debates in the latter part of the twentieth century and have had a very significant impact on the field of sustainable development. A major consequence of these overpopulation paradigms were policies to reduce women's fertility, including in some cases through coercive population control measures. While the global policy framework now recognizes that population policies must be anchored in sexual and reproductive health and reproductive rights, the persistence of concerns regarding overpopulation continue to shape population policies that are narrowly focused on reducing women's fertility.

The basic premise of degradation narratives is that in rural parts of developing countries, population pressure coupled with poverty is the main cause of land degradation. In other words, the poor are primarily responsible for destroying their own environments (Fairhead, 2001; Hartmann, 2010). These narratives have their roots in colonial policies that justified land expropriation by blaming native agricultural practices and population pressures for soil erosion, deforestation and desertification (Fairhead and Leach, 1996; Adams, 2004). Later they were used to justify external interventions such as the top-down implementation of rural development projects and population control programmes (Williams, 1995; Roe, 1995).

Degradation narratives have expanded to include a negative view of migration. In this perspective, after poor people deplete their immediate environments, many migrate to other marginal lands, setting in motion the same vicious downward spiral. From the 1990s onwards, this perspective included the poor who flock to already overcrowded cities and,

most recently, so-called climate refugees — the new environmental refugees (Doyle and Chaturvedi, 2011).

The concept of carrying capacity is central to the view of population growth exceeding the planet's capacity to produce food and thus degrading the environment and causing wars, and has also been deployed in order to influence policy efforts to limit population growth in developing countries (Sayre, 2008; Vogt, 1948). Similarly, the idea of the S-curve, where animal, plant and human populations grow exponentially until they meet environmental resistance and then decline, has also reinforced the concept of saturation point as the upper level at which no further population increase can occur (Odum, 1953).

The tragedy of the commons approach, based on concerns for the planet's carrying capacity, has advocated for population control and private property rights and has had an enduring impact on policy responses and debates (Hardin, 1968). Yet people have been managing common resources cooperatively for centuries and are able to negotiate successfully the tensions between private gain and the public, and environmental, good. For example, work on common pool resources has documented many cases where individuals create stable institutions of self-government that make and enforce rules which protect natural resources and provide mutual protection against risk (Ostrom, 2000).

Gender relations are often critical in processes of managing common pool resources. As Ostrom explained: "it is certainly the case that when women are active participants in making rules and affecting the way a commons operates that the long-term impacts are likely to be better and the equity of outcomes is likely to be much better ... In those settings where gender inequity decreases, there is certainly a much broader consideration of future generations and less concern about immediate monetary payoff" (Ostrom, in May and Summerfield, 2012).

The ideas and narratives of overpopulation have had a far-reaching impact on policy responses in relation to population, health, development, environment and migration, often with significant consequences for the enjoyment of human rights and gender equality. While sustainable development advocates have acknowledged the role of inequality and other factors, some continue to see population pressure as the most important cause of both poverty and environmental degradation (Myers and Kent, 1995).

Against this background, the efforts of gender equality advocates and women's movements led to a significant change in the approach to population at the International Conference on Population and Development, held in Cairo in 1994. The Conference represented a major international policy shift from population control to women's empowerment and a broader sexual and reproductive health and reproductive rights agenda. The Programme of Action adopted at the Conference, or "Cairo consensus", was endorsed by most of the world's governments and condemned the use of coercion, including incentives and disincentives in family planning provision. Instead, it promoted voluntary family planning as a part of reproductive health, including maternal care, sexuality education and prevention of sexually transmitted infections.

The Programme of Action of the International Conference on Population and Development maintained that rapid population growth was a major cause of poverty and environmental degradation, and that reduced fertility rates were necessary for sustainable development.

At the same time, it advocated for a positive agenda of women's empowerment and broader reproductive health programmes as solutions to high birth rates, instead of the top-down, target-driven family planning programmes of the past.

Despite the pledges adopted at the International Conference on Population and Development, commitments on sexual and reproductive health and reproductive rights were not subsequently fully reflected in the Millennium Development Goals. Initially, the Goals did not include a specific target for advancing reproductive health and rights, and instead included target 5 (now 5A), which called for reducing maternal mortality. Target 5B was added in 2005, at the 5-year review point, to promote universal access to reproductive health care. Yet Goal 5, with both targets A and B, narrows the Programme of Action of the International Conference on Population and Development from a broad sexual and reproductive health and reproductive rights agenda to an emphasis on reproduction. As sexual and reproductive health and rights are important for preventing maternal mortality and morbidity, this narrow agenda has stymied even the achievement of the limited aims of Goal 5 (see E/CN.6/2014/3). By only focusing narrowly on maternal health, the role of women shifted from "agents of social change, and the subjects of rights", as envisaged in the Programme of Action, to "child-bearers and caretakers" who are "limited to their pregnancy status" (Yamin and Boulanger, 2013). Following the emphasis on pregnancy, international funding streams, which were already scarce, have been channelled largely towards maternal and child health provision, while other aspects of sexual

The ideas and narratives of overpopulation have had a far-reaching impact on policy responses in relation to population, health, development, environment and migration, often with significant consequences for the enjoyment of human rights and gender equality and reproductive health and rights, including contraception, experienced a decrease in funding (Yamin and Boulanger, 2013).

2. Patterns of consumption and production

For proponents of overpopulation paradigms, scarcity is a foregone conclusion and driving down population growth rates is the only solution. Technology and market enthusiasts are more optimistic. In the case of food, for example, they put their faith in the expansion of agricultural trade and production (see chap. IV, on food security). Between these two poles, however, are a range of issues that merit consideration for policy development.

Acknowledging the problems with the narratives concerning population and the environment does not deny the very real pressures population growth can put on the availability of vital resources, namely, food, water, sanitation, energy, housing, jobs, social services, especially in an era of rapid urbanization and climate change. Projecting population growth and greenhouse gas emissions to the year 2100 in one integrated model showed that slowing population growth would reduce future emissions: "by the end of the century, the effect of slower population growth would be ... significant, reducing total emissions from fossil fuel use by 37-41 per cent" (O'Neill and others, 2010). However, the problem here is equating larger populations to greater emissions, without paying attention to the more significant issue of consumption levels or the distribution of consumption.

The problem here is equating larger populations to greater emissions, without paying attention to the more significant issue of consumption level or the distribution of consumption

While carbon legacies, the projected carbon emissions of descendants, deriving from the fertility of individual women, can be significant when juxtaposed with projected greenhouse gas emissions, there is generally an inverse relationship between individual childbearing and per capita greenhouse gas emissions. In other words, countries where women bear the fewest children are most often those with the higher rates of per capita greenhouse gas emissions and the highest carbon legacies (Murtaugh and Schlax, 2009).

Instead, focusing on consumption shows that "it is not the growth in (urban or rural) populations that drives the growth in greenhouse gas (GHG) emissions but rather, the growth in consumers and in their levels of consumption" (Satterthwaite, 2009). In developing countries with rapid population growth, those in higher income classes are most able to consume resources, such as fossil fuels for vehicles and household electricity, making high levels of greenhouse gas emissions per capita primarily the domain of the affluent. In the case of high-income developed countries as well, richer households emit far more carbon than lower income ones (Boyce and Riddle, 2007).

Developing economies, which represent 80 per cent of the world's population, accounted for 73 per cent of the growth in global emissions in 2004. But they accounted for only 41 per cent of global emissions in that year, and only 23 per cent of global cumulative emissions since the start of the industrial revolution (Raupach and others, 2007). These perspectives underscore the need to evaluate the links between population growth and climate change in the context of patterns of consumption and production and global equity. Beyond sheer numbers of people, population policies and responses to climate change must take a long-term perspective on emissions and focus on changing patterns of production and consumption. Indeed, the principle of common but differentiated responsibilities concerns the joint responsibility of all countries to protect the environment, while recognizing the need to

A counsellor from a reproductive health NGO, Pakistan, talks to a woman about her rights

take into account the different circumstances, particularly the contribution of developed and developing countries to environmental degradation and the different abilities of countries to address the problem.

3. Reducing fertility rates and "missing women"

From the late 1960s to the 1990s, reducing fertility in poor countries was a major component of bilateral and multilateral agency policies and programmes, and was also vigorously pursued by national population planning in developing countries.[37] The urgency of limiting birth rates led to coercive practices, such as forced sterilization and pressuring or bribing women to use higher-risk contraceptives without adequate informed consent or medical support. This meant that family planning became an instrument to control population growth rather than to protect and promote "the basic right of all couples and individuals to decide freely and responsibly the number, spacing and timing of their children and to have the information and means to do so, and the right to attain the highest standard of sexual and reproductive health".[9]

Framing the population issue in relation to resource and environmental pressures was a fundamental factor in building public consensus for population control interventions (Connelly, 2008; Hartmann, 1995). The constitution of China mandates that the government support family planning and that individual couples practice it. The one-child policy, introduced in the late 1970s, has been implemented through a system of economic and social incentives and disincentives, along with free contraceptive services (United Nations, 2002). The application of the policy varies by province and between rural and urban areas, as the decisions regarding implementation are made at the provincial level. For example, outside of cities, two children are generally permitted and three children are permitted for some minority ethnic groups (Hesketh, Lu, and Wei Xing, 2005). Decades after the introduction of the policy, at the fifteenth session of the Conference of the Parties to the United Nations Framework Convention on Climate Change, held in Copenhagen in 2009,

the Vice-Minister of the National Population and Family Planning Commission of China, Zhao Baige, noted that the country's family planning policy had prevented the birth of 400 million Chinese people and thereby reduced carbon dioxide emissions by 18 million tons per year (Xing, 2009; Feng, Cai and Gu, 2013). In Viet Nam, limiting families to two children became obligatory in the 1980s. Incentives for the use of contraception, as well as penalties for family planning violations, were introduced in an effort to promote implementation of the population policy (United Nations, 2002).

In countries with marked son preference, one-child and similar population policies have led to distorted sex ratios. Population data show a sex ratio at birth of 117 males per 100 females for China, 110 males per 100 females for Viet Nam and 111 males per 100 females for India (United Nations, 2013c). The biologically normal sex ratio at birth ranges from 102 to 106 males per 100 females (World Health Organization, 2011). Such policies have given rise to the widespread practice of sex-selective abortion, as well as the abandonment, hiding and neglect of female children. The World Bank estimates that in 2008 alone, there were an estimated 1 million fewer girls in China and 250,000 fewer girls in India than expected as a result of such practices (World Bank, 2012, p. 78). The one-child policy has also had negative gender outcomes for men, especially poor men in rural areas who cannot find spouses and who are stigmatized as "bare branches" (Greenhalgh, 2005).

Other contributing factors to this positive association between women's empowerment and fertility decline include women's access to gainful employment outside the home and the opportunity to earn an independent income. There is ample statistical evidence, based on comparisons between countries and regions, that link women's education to the lowering of fertility (Sen, 1999). Recent work by Chinese demographers indicates that most of China's fertility transition was accomplished in the decade of the 1970s, before the implementation of the one-child policy. The country's total fertility

In many low- and middle-income countries, sustained growth coupled with better services and economic opportunities for women over the past decades has been linked with declines in the total fertility rate, improvements in education for girls and women and greater labour force participation

rate dropped from 5.8 in 1970 to 2.8 in 1979, and would likely have continued to decline even in the absence of the one-child policy, as a result of mortality decline, increases in education and rapid social and economic changes (Feng, Cai and Gu, 2013). What such analysis suggests is that "economic development may be far from 'the best contraceptive', but social development — especially women's employment and education — can be very effective indeed" (Sen, 1999). In southern Indian states such as Kerala and Tamil Nadu, fertility rates dropped dramatically between 1979 and 1991 (from 3.0 to 1.8, and from 3.5 to 2.2, respectively), thanks to their remarkable achievements in terms of women's literacy rates, high levels of female labour force participation and relatively low infant mortality, as well as an active, but non-coercive family planning programme (Sen, 1999). This contrasts with the record of other Indian states and also other countries, which despite heavy-handed family planning methods, failed to achieve similar outcomes. "The regional contrasts within India strongly argue for voluntarism (based inter alia, on the active and educated participation of women), as opposed to coercion" (Sen, 1999).

These findings are corroborated by more recent assessments from other countries and regions, which show notable declines in fertility linked to women's education and paid employment. In many low- and middle-income countries, sustained growth coupled with better services and economic opportunities for women over the past decades has been linked with declines in the total fertility rate, improvements in education for girls and women and greater labour force

participation. In Bangladesh, the economy has almost tripled in size since 1980; the total fertility rate declined from 6.9 children in 1971 to 2.3 in 2009; the number of girls in school increased from 33 per cent to 56 per cent of total enrolment between 1991 and 2005; and the labour force participation of young women between the ages of 20 and 24 increased almost two and half times between 1995 and 2000. In Colombia, the economy has grown one and a half times since 1980; the total fertility rate declined from 3.2 children in 1986 to 2.4 in 2005; women now have higher completion rates than men for primary, secondary and tertiary education; and from 1980 to 2004, the labour force participation of women in the 13 largest cities went from being the second lowest in the region to the second highest. In the Islamic Republic of Iran, the economy has almost doubled since 1980; from 1979 to 2009, there was the fastest decline in total fertility rate in the world, from 6.9 children to 1.8 (below-replacement level); 1.2 girls are enrolled in primary school for every boy, the number of women in secondary school has doubled, and women make up more than 50 per cent of total university students and 68 per cent of those in science; and at present, women represent 30 per cent of the labour force (World Bank, 2012).

These diverse country examples indicate the importance of a comprehensive approach to gender equality and the realization of women's human rights and capabilities, including the provision of quality education, health services and access to decent work, along with the availability of accessible family planning services, as effective means of fertility reduction.

D/ BROADENING THE POPULATION AGENDA

This chapter has identified many of the challenges posed by the enduring legacy of population paradigms and models that are deeply rooted in development thinking and practice. They focus on women's fertility as both the cause of and the solution to serious global problems, from environmental destruction and climate change to economic instability and political conflict. The narrow focus on overpopulation as a driver of environmental challenges distracts from unsustainable patterns and levels of production and consumption and inequities between and within countries.

Population policies must be broadened from fertility reduction to the realization of women's and girls' human rights and capabilities. Sustainable development cannot be achieved unless all women and girls enjoy universal access to sexual and reproductive health and rights over the life cycle, enabling them to make free and informed decisions about sex and reproduction. This requires the development of policies and legal frameworks and the strengthening of health systems to provide universally accessible quality sexual and reproductive health services, information and education across the life cycle, including on safe and effective methods of modern contraception, safe abortion, comprehensive sexuality education and maternal health care.

For the full realization of sexual and reproductive health and rights, governments have a responsibility to ensure that along with other essential services, health services are available, accessible, acceptable and of appropriate quality for all. This requires targeted measures to address the structural inequalities, stigma and discrimination that limit access to health services for women and girls. Ensuring access to quality education at all levels and access to decent work is also essential for broadening the population agenda.

Sustainable development cannot be achieved unless all women and girls enjoy universal access to sexual and reproductive health and rights over the life cycle, enabling them to make free and informed decisions about sex and reproduction

CHAPTER /6

INVESTMENTS FOR GENDER-RESPONSIVE
SUSTAINABLE DEVELOPMENT

A/ INTRODUCTION

This chapter develops an agenda for sustainable development, with particular emphasis on local priorities, poverty eradication and gender equality. It extends the argument of the previous chapters that sustainable development should enhance the capabilities of women and girls, so they are able "to lead the lives they value — and have reason to value" (Sen, 1999). Capability is akin to freedom, meaning the freedom to lead a particular life as opposed to another. Because the capabilities framework emphasizes choice in addition to outcomes of well-being (Nussbaum, 2000), it is only indirectly linked to specific bundles of goods and services. Yet in order to deliver tangible improvements for women and girls, investments must be directed towards sectors from which they can benefit the most. The term "investment" is used to denote financial, social and institutional efforts aimed at creating future benefits for humans and their environments. This chapter highlights four domains with a particularly strong potential to transform the lives of women and girls: domestic water, safe sanitation, clean(er) cookstoves and domestic electricity services. Expanding access to these goods and services can improve gender equality directly and specifically, because women suffer disproportionately from their absence (Antonopoulos and Hirway, 2010; Anenberg and others, 2013). There is ample evidence, for example, that the physical burden of food, fuel and water collection reduces women's capabilities relative to their own potential and relative to those of men (e.g., Cecelski, 1984; Ray, 2007).

Access to water, sanitation, clean cookstoves and electricity are the backbone of a decent quality of life and the basis on which a range of other life choices can or cannot be made. And yet there is significant underinvestment in these areas, relative to the global need. The four domains are directly connected to environmental sustainability.

For example, high rates of open defecation, which contribute to water pollution and health hazards, are directly linked to inadequate sanitation facilities. Greater investments in these areas are therefore needed, for both social and environmental sustainability. However, not all investments in these sectors are sustainable and gender-responsive. The chapter proposes two dimensions for assessing investments in these areas from the perspective of gender equality and sustainable development:

(a) The risks and benefits of technologies, innovations and societal investments, including the gendered distribution of those risks and benefits;

(b) The extent to which the human rights and capabilities of women, especially those of poor women and girls, can be (or have been) advanced as a result of such investments.

Measuring the extent to which women's and girls' capabilities are enhanced through specific investments is not an easy task. Improvements in under-five female mortality and gender parity in secondary education are useful indicators for assessing and evaluating transformative investments in water, sanitation, cookstoves and electricity: they are particularly relevant for low-income communities or countries; they are a prerequisite to many other capabilities; and they are routinely measured in a large number of countries. In addition, investments should be assessed based on their potential and performance with regards to reducing unpaid care work for women and girls. While this indicator is not routinely calculated, time-use data for many countries exist, and could be used to measure progress. If investment outcomes are measured in terms of capabilities, so should the decision-making processes that bring them about. Most importantly, sustainable

Strong public action by civil society and the state is required in order to expand the capabilities of all and protect environmental resources

development investments (local or national) should ensure that those who bear the risks of the intervention also hold the right to shape it.

While the past decades have brought significant improvements in the technological possibilities at the core of these services, including more efficient, lower-carbon and lower-cost options, they cannot go to scale on the basis of technological interventions alone. Nor is there a guarantee that improved technologies for use by women will automatically improve women's lives. The vast literature on access to basic services for the poor strongly suggests that universal and gender-responsive access cannot be ensured by voluntary mechanisms alone (i.e., through the market or the non-governmental sector). Strong public

action by civil society and the state is required in order to expand the capabilities of all and protect environmental resources.

The chapter explores four concepts. Section B turns to the question of how to assess (ex ante) or evaluate (ex post) a sustainable development intervention through the lens of gender equality. Drawing on the literatures on risk and risk perceptions, and on the operationalization of capabilities and well-being, some assessment criteria for socially transformative investments are suggested. Each of the four investment domains is in section C, along with technological and social approaches towards providing basic levels of service. There are considerable political and institutional barriers to providing services to low-income populations at scale, and in particular for ensuring gender equality or environmental integrity in their provision. Section D focuses on the institutional contexts that may enable sustainable development pathways. It highlights the relevance of civil society alliances that are needed to support social investments at the necessary scales. Section E covers ways and means of financing such investments.

B/ ASSESSING TRANSFORMATIVE INVESTMENTS FOR GENDER EQUALITY

1. Assessing the risks of investments

Innovative technologies and the programmes that implement them always have risks. For every category of development investment, therefore, it is important to ask what kinds of risks are being taken and who will assume the potential costs. The rights and risks approach of

the World Commission on Dams (2000) is useful in this regard. It has been valuable in laying out a framework for responsible public investments for dam-building, and can be usefully applied to other sectors. The World Commission clearly distinguished risk bearers from rights bearers, arguing that those who have risks imposed on them (risk bearers) often do not have rights with respect to investment decisions that are commensurate with their risks.

The members of the World Commission on Dams argued that the differential risk profiles and perceptions within and across communities call for transparent discussions with all the affected and interested parties, recognizing that the two may not be the same, and acknowledging that unforeseen consequences are always possible. The broader risk literature on technology and social acceptance has indeed shown that risk cannot be understood simply as a probability distribution of outcomes. People bring to their risk assessments not only the attributes of a technology, but also their cultural and political frames of reference and their social uncertainties and fears. These subjective and situated perspectives are not merely a matter of better communication of technical risks; they require analysis of the multiple criteria by which the risks are perceived (Stirling, 1998). For sustainable development, the rights and risks framework, with its emphasis on risk perception, risk distribution and the voluntary or involuntary nature of the risks, is especially important for large-scale and irreversible investments. In the case of large dams, for instance, on which the report of the World Commission was based, it was shown that affected and displaced communities often bore the risks of dam-building, but rarely enjoyed the right to shape decisions or benefit from new employment opportunities. Women and others without legal title to land were not allocated land in compensation for submerged holdings. This relatively unfavourable gender outcome, the World Commission argued, could apply to many investments other than dams (such as roads), when the risk bearers were not the rights holders.

2. Assessing the outcomes of investments

It is important to be able to assess potential investments in terms of their impact on gender equality and the local priorities and needs of the poorest people. If investment X is going to be promoted over investment Y, there must be clear criteria for estimating the impact before investing, or evaluating the impact after the investment

has been made. As a core criterion, investments in the name of sustainable development should be assessed against their ability to enhance the capabilities of women and girls. No development pathway can be considered "sustainable" if it reduces women's capabilities. Thus if an investment in a low-carbon and energy-efficient option intended for the poor inadvertently increases unpaid care work for women, then it is not on a sustainable development pathway. This is not to deny the clear and urgent need for decarbonizing the global economy, but rather to argue, as outlined in chapter 2, that an emissions-centric or planetary-boundaries view of sustainability is inadequate from a local development or gender equality perspective. A capabilities approach to assessing investments requires a shift from the income-plus-environmental-footprint yardstick through which sustainable development is most often measured. Several measures have been put forth in order to assess capability enhancement.

One possibility for measuring women's capability enhancement, while keeping the measure practical and selective, is to choose among the indicators that already form part of the Human Development Index of the United Nations Development Programme, such as life expectancy and gender bias.[38] The Human Development Index is derived from Sen's influential capabilities and functionings approach (Sen, 1985) and can be seen as a way to operationalize capabilities. The Index as a whole is somewhat generic and large-scale; clearly, specific socioeconomic circumstances and priorities should dictate which indicators of capability are most relevant. For instance, for community-based investments in sanitation, an education indicator (such as secondary school enrolment for girls) might be the metric of evaluation. For investments in clean domestic energy for the very poor, female and infant mortality may be a more suitable metric. The indicators of interest should be measured for the overall population, but should also be measured for the lowest quintiles. They can be measured at multiple scales, for the state as a whole or for a single local intervention.

Greater efforts are needed from Member States to prioritize the systematic collection, reporting and analysis of data on the minimum set of gender indicators adopted by the United Nations Statistical Commission

As a means of illustrating the approach, the female under-five mortality rate and the ratio of female to male enrolment in secondary education could be considered potentially useful capability measures in the context of the four priority areas analysed in this chapter (Saith and Harriss-White, 1999; Unterhalter, 2013). Such indicators are relevant for low-income communities or countries. Along with anthropometric indicators of nutrition, under-five mortality ratios and secondary school enrolment correspond to intrinsically important capabilities and are the precondition to the realization of many other human rights and capabilities. They are also realistic indicators given that child mortality and school enrolment data, imperfect though they may be, are routinely measured in a large number of countries. Other indicators could serve the purpose as well.

The enrolment measure is the female-to-male ratio as this is a direct indicator of parity; however, the simple rate of female participation in secondary education is also a plausible capability metric. Secondary school enrolment is emphasized over primary schooling: the literature has convincingly shown that more years in school are associated with girls being able to articulate their rights and better protect themselves and their families against illness (Unterhalter, 2013).

Two criteria may be a small number for the purpose of measuring gender equality across multiple domains. However, these are proposed as illustrative and important, rather than as sufficient, constituents of a sustainable pathway; their selection is entirely context-specific. It is expected that actual investments will be assessed through additional environmental and economic criteria. But selectivity and simplicity are essential for indicators to gain policy traction. Indeed, just one indicator may be a good assessment criterion for specific contexts, depending on the pre-investment baseline conditions.

An indicator for gender-responsive development that is indeed crucial is the reduction of unpaid care work. Every economy is dependent on the unpaid care economy (Razavi, 2007), comprising cooking, cleaning, elder care, childcare and community-based volunteering. In low-income economies, care work also includes fetching water and fuel, often over long distances. Unpaid work is heavily feminized, and the burden of unpaid work may increase or decrease as a result of ostensibly sustainable interventions. They may even be deemed sustainable because they rely on uncounted unpaid work; much-lauded interventions such as rainwater harvesting and community-based resource management have been critiqued on this ground (Jackson, 1993; Kabeer, 2005). Reduction of unpaid care work, particularly in low-income households, is essential if women and girls are to develop the full range of their capabilities. This indicator is not routinely calculated in the Human Development Index. Although countries are increasingly collecting time-use data, the lack of data in several areas such as women's experiences of poverty, unpaid care work, women's participation in decision-making at all levels and women's access to, ownership of and control of assets and productive resources, limits the assessment of gender equality and women's capabilities. Greater efforts are needed from Member States to prioritize the systematic collection, reporting and analysis of data on the minimum set of gender indicators adopted by the United Nations Statistical Commission.[39]

C/ CATEGORIES OF INVESTMENT FOR GENDER-RESPONSIVE SUSTAINABLE DEVELOPMENT

Reliable domestic water supplies, clean and dignified sanitation, cleaner cookstoves and domestic electricity services are all basic categories. Every person, regardless of their age, gender or class, needs to drink water, breathe, eat cooked food, urinate and defecate, and see in the dark. Investments in these areas affect everyone every day, and therefore contribute to the fulfilment of capabilities and of human rights. They are the determinants of health and livelihood for all and the backbone of what has been called the "environmentalism of the poor" (Martínez-Alier, 2002). They are particularly critical for poor women given their social responsibilities in meeting the needs of other household members as well as their own. They should therefore be at the centre of policy efforts to achieve sustainable development.

All four categories of investment have spillover effects that benefit users as well as non-users (e.g., access to safe sanitation for women increases overall community health and efficient cookstoves improve household health as well as household budgets). Unsafe water, unsafe sanitation and indoor air pollution from solid fuels, account for some 11 per cent of deaths in low-income countries (WHO, 2009). All four investments have a technological core, but investing in technology alone cannot ensure that innovations are taken to a transformative scale. All four have significant positive externalities, meaning that the social benefits from their provision tend to exceed private benefits. Therefore markets are likely to underdeliver these goods and services, making them candidates for investments in the public domain. This does not preclude private sector participation but calls for coordinated efforts to direct private investments towards broader social goals, through context-specific subsidies and regulations. Investment in all four categories can either be channelled along unsustainable pathways that may not promote gender equality, or along more sustainable and equitable innovation pathways, through which capabilities may be improved. Focusing on these categories, therefore, does not imply that these will inevitably lead to gender equality, nor that these are the only worthwhile investments for sustainable development. Many investments can be transformative for poverty eradication and for gender equality, such as good infrastructure, mobile technologies for development, or financial inclusion for the unbanked. The emphasis is on investment categories that are likely to improve gender equality directly and specifically, especially for poorer women, because they are disproportionately burdened with poor health

The emphasis is on investment categories that are likely to improve gender equality directly and specifically, especially for poorer women, because they are disproportionately burdened with poor health and unpaid care work in the absence of such investment and unpaid care work in the absence of such investment (Antonopoulos and Hirway, 2010).

Sanitation investments in urban South Asia or Africa that provide a low toilet-to-user ratio often preclude women from using them, because they cannot stand in long queues in the morning or walk to facilities at night. On the other hand, many community-led total sanitation initiatives from Africa, such as from Kenya and Sierra Leone, have shown that women readily assume leadership roles in encouraging latrine construction and in the community mobilization activities that community-led total sanitation needs (Hickling and Bevan, 2010). Several improved cookstove interventions, in China, India and Kenya, have simultaneously improved household air pollution and potentially improved women's respiratory health, though the latter has been challenging to measure. An especially successful programme is China's national improved stoves programme to replace coal-burning stoves (Sinton and others, 2004), discussed in more detail below.

1. Water

Some 748 million people worldwide are without access to improved water sources (WHO/UNICEF, 2014), defined by WHO as water from a protected well, protected spring, collected rainwater, boreholes or tap. Diarrhoea from microbial contamination (even in "improved" water) claims the lives of 1.6 million children under five every years (WHO/UNICEF, 2006). Many innovative approaches are being developed and disseminated towards improving water quality. This section focuses on reliable access to adequate and improved quantities of water for domestic use. Especially for women in developing countries, basic access comes first.

Social expectations dictate that women and girls are the primary water carriers for their families; in over 70 per cent of households where water has to be fetched, women and girls do the fetching (WHO/UNICEF, 2012). Where rural water sources are distant, women

walk up to two hours to fetch water. Where urban water is from shared standpipes they may wait in line for over an hour (see Ray, 2007). Survey data for 25 sub-Saharan countries indicate that women spend a total of 16 million hours a day collecting water (WHO/UNICEF, 2012); the more distant the source of water, the less water the household uses. Case studies from around the world show that water-related time poverty translates to lost income for women and lost schooling for girls (UNDP, 2006). In addition, high levels of mental stress result when water rights are insecure. All this fetching and carrying causes cumulative wear-and-tear to the neck, spine, back and knees; in effect, a woman's body becomes part of the water-delivery infrastructure, doing the work of pipes.

In many developing countries, urban access to improved water is higher than rural access, and access at the top quintile is significantly higher than at the bottom quintile. These trends are commensurate with the Human Development Report of 2006, which stated unequivocally that lack of access to water stemmed from inequality and lack of rights and not from some generalized notion of scarcity (UNDP, 2006), echoing the analysis in chapter 4 on the right to food.

Even in urban areas, where the access percentages are usually higher, the reliability, quality and affordability of access for the lowest quintiles are all insecure. Continuous piped water has the greatest health benefits and lowest drudgery costs, but is technologically and financially viable only for densely populated communities. Piped water with a sewer connection for developing countries would have required $136 billion a year from 2000 to 2015 in order to meet the target of the Millennium Development Goals; meeting the target using cheaper supply technologies, including borewells, low-cost pipes and roof-water capture, and without adding point-of-use treatments to improve water quality, has been estimated at under $2 billion annually (Hutton, Haller and Bartram,

2007). According to the WHO/UNICEF Joint Monitoring Programme on Water Supply and Sanitation,[40] the global water access target for the Goals was met by 2013, but this target falls short of universal access; falls short of water safe to drink; has been achieved largely through urban rather than rural access; and is quite compatible with continued time poverty for women, high costs of access and other indicators of water poverty (e.g., highly variable water quality, low reliability of water access source, physical burden of collecting and hauling).

In rural areas, modest quantities of water are needed not just for consumption but for livelihoods. Zwarteveen (1997) argues that an exclusive focus on the domestic water sector when discussing women's water needs overlooks the increasing number of woman-headed small farm households, and emphasizes the role of women as mothers rather than as producers as well. Rural systems that are "multiple use", meaning that they provide water for drinking and for small plots and a few cattle or goats, are more likely to respond to the range of basic needs that rural women must meet. They have a higher potential for cost recovery as they help to generate income, especially if credit is available. A drinking-water focused intervention, by contrast, such as a borehole with a pump, could have a life cycle per person per year cost of $20 to $60, with little chance of cost recovery from its low-income user base. From a pragmatic rather than human rights perspective, donors and governments are, in today's global economy, more ready to invest in schemes with partial cost recovery potential as opposed to none.

In addition to large storage-based multipurpose water projects, decentralized water-augmenting technologies exist, and have collectively reached many millions. Many of these would count as "multiple use" in today's terminology. Several of these are "modernized" traditional approaches, often community-based. The best-known example is rainwater harvesting, which is being taken to scale by communities in partnership with governments and non-governmental organizations. Another is the treadle pump, which is a foot-powered pump that extracts shallow water for domestic purposes, as well as for small farms and kitchen plots. The revival and modernization of these techniques are owed partly to recurrent droughts, and partly to efforts to counter the narrative that large dams were the only channel to water security. But a lack of funding and policy interest has prevented these approaches from reaching truly transformative scales (see Sovacool, 2012).

Everywhere, water is another word for life; access to water for poor women is one of the highest priorities of sustainable development. In this sense, the history of failed water projects in rural and urban areas is instructive. A frequently cited reason for failure is that women's voices and views were ignored before and during these efforts; and that women are the water users and therefore the ones with knowledge and stakes. Women's agency, voice and leadership are thus essential to sustainable and gender-responsive water access and must go beyond "tokenistic" participation. While it would be naïve to argue that women's leadership is either necessary or sufficient for sustainable community-level water projects, numerous case studies from Ethiopia, India, Kenya, Nepal, Pakistan, South Africa and the United Republic of Tanzania, among others, have argued that placing women at the centre of water and sanitation decisions has led to more cost-effective delivery, more households with access to water and less corruption in water

Women's agency, voice and leadership are essential to sustainable and gender-responsive water access and must go beyond "tokenistic" participation financing (Fisher, 2006; Chattopadhyay and Duflo, 2004).

2. Sanitation

Sanitation is a basic need, and yet access to improved facilities is denied to billions of people worldwide. It is important to understand that for social as well as biological reasons, women and men face different risks and have different needs with regard to sanitation. For example, girls and women may be exposed to sexual violence when accessing shared and off-site facilities, and the lack of adequate facilities in schools may keep girls away, particularly during menstruation.

"Improved" sanitation facilities, according to WHO and UNICEF, include pour flush or flush toilets into a sewer, ventilated improved pits and composting toilets, through the use of which pathogenic waste is likely to be removed from human contact. Many different toilet designs, from the simple pit with slab, to more complex but locally producible dry (ecological) toilets, exist for low-income households (Nelson and Murray, 2008). But over 2.5 billion people still have no access to an improved latrine; of these, 761 million use shared facilities, which the Joint Monitoring Programme for Water Supply and Sanitation of WHO and UNICEF does not consider "improved". Open defecation rates have gone down in all developing countries (WHO/UNICEF, 2013), but it remains the norm for over 1 billion people, 90 per cent of whom are rural residents.

Open defecation is a severe public health risk as well as an environmental hazard, causing widespread diarrhoeal disease and water pollution. Sanitation programmes are gaining increasing attention, relative to the previous neglect of such programmes in comparison with drinking water programmes, and are promoted vigorously by health researchers, by governments in concert with local communities and by international non-governmental organizations. It is still the case that for every $4 spent on water and sanitation programmes, sanitation receives about $1 (WHO, 2012). But a sea change has occurred in recent years with respect to recognizing sanitation as indispensable for health and development.

Basic sanitation that is clean, affordable to construct and to maintain, and safe to access, is a particularly transformative investment for women's and girls' capabilities. Women need more privacy than men when they use the facilities because of social norms, need more time in the toilet than men do (because they must sit or squat), need physical safety when they access toilets outside of the dwelling, and may need multiple daily visits during their menstrual period. For these reasons, access to sanitation access is as germane to gender equality and dignity as access to water. As with water access, sanitation access in low-income countries is highly unequal; as with water, urban coverage rates for sanitation are significantly higher than rural coverage rates (WHO/UNICEF, 2013). Even within rural regions, access is lowest for communities far away from main roads. Overall, it is estimated that children in the poorest quintiles of low-income countries (in South Asia and sub-Saharan Africa) suffer up to 20 times the health burden of inadequate sanitation as children in the top quintiles within those same countries.

New directions in sanitation research and promotion have largely been focused on extending access through developing new technologies, encouraging toilet uptake, improving markets for sanitation products, encouraging a larger role for non-state actors and discouraging open defecation (Black and Fawcett, 2008; water.org;[41] Bill and Melinda Gates Foundation). Several donor efforts (e.g., the Gates Foundation's "Reinvent the Toilet" initiative) and government-community partnership efforts (e.g., community-led total sanitation campaigns) are focused on sustainable sanitation for the poor. Community-led total sanitation emphasizes rural sanitation, as this reflects both the origins of the concept in rural areas (Kar and Chambers, 2008) as well as where open defecation mostly occurs. It is a subsidy-free approach to community mobilization for sanitation that encourages people to build their own toilets/latrines with local resources to stop open defecation. Community-led total sanitation encourages women to take leadership roles, but also builds on traditional notions of women as the keepers of cleanliness and order in the family and can add to women's existing labour (Mehta and Movik, 2011). But there are also city-based examples of urban sanitation with community leadership at their centre, using sanitation as a community-building as well as toilet-building exercise, from South Asia, Central America and Southern Africa. These methods, which were once pilot projects but are now becoming mainstream, represent a major change from previous supply-driven and facilities-driven approaches. It is still unclear if these demand-driven means can be sustained over time in multiple settings, or if they can adapt to the political economies of different countries well enough to go to scale (e.g., Harris, Kooy and Jones, 2011, on Viet Nam).

The definition of improved (or reinvented) latrines in all these efforts remains hardware-oriented, saying little about wastewater treatment before disposal or sludge removal if the toilet is a dry toilet. Untreated sewage and faecal sludge from overflowing pits are highly polluting and unsustainable. If improved sanitation required sewage to be treated before its discharge into the environment, 4.1 billion rather than 2.6 billion people would be counted as unserved (Baum, Luh and Bartram, 2013). Sustainable toilet designs therefore have to include not only the reduction of open

defecation, but also the disposal and reuse of pathogenic waste (Nelson and Murray, 2008). Financing sanitation at the required scale remains an unmet global challenge, with great uncertainty in existing cost estimates and almost no estimates of spending by private households. Hutton and Bartram (2008) estimate that about $36 billion (2008 US dollars) annually will need to be invested for 10 years to meet (and maintain) the Millennium Development Goals target of reducing by half the population without access to improved sanitation. If primary treatment of toilet waste and long-term maintenance costs are added, the cost of "sustainable sanitation" can be 5 to 20 times the cost of building the latrine alone. Innovative social enterprises that safely convert human waste into reusable sludge or renewable energy are being piloted at the scale of urban slums (e.g., Sanergy),[42] exploiting the possibilities for cost recovery from productive reuse, but these efforts are still at the pilot stages.

The emphasis on eliminating open defecation is absolutely critical. But it is not enough for sustainable or gender-responsive sanitation. Clean and secure sanitation can enable girls' education, women's mobility and women's and girls' physical and sexual security. However, gender equality means that toilet programmes have to go beyond addressing defecation and disease management and take equally seriously the requirements of privacy, safety and menstrual hygiene management. Menstrual hygiene has often been neglected in national and international sanitation promotions; it is only now being acknowledged as the critical programmatic gap for the post-2015 development targets (WHO/UNICEF, 2013). Sanitation facilities and products that are safe and private enable girls to stay in school and reduce their discomfort and potential shame during menstruation. Evidence from India, Nepal, Nigeria and the United Republic of Tanzania indicates that a lack of sanitary facilities and clean cloths during menstruation keeps girls from school, and that clean safe toilets, as well as menstrual hygiene education, keep girls in school. Other studies from India

Menstrual hygiene has often been neglected in national and international sanitation promotions; it is only now being acknowledged as the critical programmatic gap for the post-2015 development targets and Kenya show that poor menstrual hygiene and changing facilities embarrass girls, keep them from physical activity during recess, keep them home and that improved and affordable sanitary products and privacy improve the experience of the school year and also quality of life overall (House, Mahon and Cavill, 2012; McMahon and others, 2011; Shah and others, 2013). In short, men and women have very different sanitation needs, for biological and social reasons. Investments in this area have to be designed and implemented with these bodily needs and the social norms that surround them as a central concern, and this means sanitation uptake programmes cannot be focused on the prevention of open defecation alone.

3. Cookstoves

It is still the norm for women to do the daily cooking for their families. It is a central part of the unpaid care economy. Women and their children, especially younger ones who are with them all the time, therefore suffer disproportionately from exposure to harmful smoke emitted from biomass-burning cookstoves. The time spent collecting fuelwood or charcoal, also a job mainly delegated to women in developing countries, is onerous and sometimes dangerous, for the women and also for the children who often accompany them. In addition, rural households are highly labour-constrained during peak agricultural seasons, and the time to collect fuelwood has high opportunity costs.

Women spend many hours per day searching for fuel and cooking over open flames that emit harmful smoke. They are therefore disproportionately affected by dirty and inefficient cooking practices and reliance on biomass fuels (Global Alliance for Clean Cookstoves, 2013). Globally, almost 3 billion people rely on solid fuels for cooking and heating; 78 per cent of this population is rural, according to Sustainable Energy for All (see www.se4all.org). Biomass-burning traditional cookstoves (i.e., stoves using wood, charcoal, animal manure or crop residues), especially when used indoors, are

the primary contributor to household air pollution. Globally, such pollution is responsible for over 4 million deaths, and household air pollution and ambient air pollution, jointly, are now the leading global environmental health risk. In South Asia and China, solid-fuel cookstoves, which are biomass-based in India but significantly coal-based in China, are the single largest contributor to household air pollution. The cumulative burdens from diseases, from black carbon and inhaled particulate matter, are manifest in respiratory infections, lung inflammation, low birthweight and cardiac events (Fullerton, Bruce and Gordon, 2008).

The health and income benefits and time savings if households can switch to cleaner-burning and more efficient cookstoves are important to communities overall. As is the case with water and sanitation, this gives them positive externalities well beyond the benefits for individual women. In South Asia and sub-Saharan Africa, for example, a large share of ambient (not just indoor) particulate matter is attributed to cooking with solid fuels.

Investing at scale in efficient solid-fuel stoves, especially in rural and peri urban regions, is simultaneously a gender-responsive and a sustainable-pathway investment. For health reasons and to prevent indoor air pollution, it would be better to switch away from cookstoves altogether and into cleaner fuels such as liquefied petroleum gas or natural gas, but this is a more ambitious proposition.

Relative to data on water and sanitation, the data by country and by quintile on access to efficient cookstoves are sparse (see Anenberg and others, 2013). In part this is because clean cookstoves are only just becoming a significant focus of public spending or routinely collected public data. National energy policies and poverty reduction strategy papers very often focus on electrification and do not adequately reflect the importance of cooking energy. The exception thus far was China's massive and organized national improved stoves programme, which has since been discontinued, but which introduced 180 million improved stoves (Sinton and others, 2004) while it lasted.

Despite growing policy attention, public investment in cleaner cookstoves remains inadequate. The first factor affecting support for cleaner cookstoves is that the effects of cookstove interventions in the field have been widely varied, some being assessed as having had no effect, others having contributed to modest health improvements, which are difficult to quantify, or to lower than anticipated improvements in indoor air pollution (see Anenberg and others, 2013). The designs and combustion efficiencies of "clean" cookstoves themselves vary widely, from those that include a chimney so that the smoke is pushed outdoors to those that simply use less fuel but retain particulate pollution indoors. The income effects of efficient stoves are more likely to be consistently positive, as many improved stoves burn between 30 per cent and 60 per cent less fuel than their unimproved counterparts; this can be a significant saving for rural households that spend nearly 10 per cent of their monthly income on energy (Miah and others, 2010).

The second consideration is that producing cookstoves that women want to use and marketing these to low-income families has been a challenge. Most cookstove interventions, even when they report satisfaction with the stoves and use of the stoves, also report the continued use of the traditional stove for staple foods (whose taste apparently changes with improved stoves). In addition, there is anecdotal evidence that women are unwilling to give up the convenience of two stoves, despite the benefits of consistently using the efficient one. This form of device "stacking" makes it harder to see health impacts and also harder to sell new stoves. In the cooking arena especially, men and women may value different aspects of clean stoves. It has been hypothesized that women value stove aesthetics and smoke-free environments more than men, who are concerned about timely meals and the traditional taste of food. Such views are not necessarily in conflict, but they present marketing challenges. It is estimated that 166 million households now use relatively inexpensive improved stoves, with 116 million in China and 22 million in South Asia. Though at-scale change remains elusive, encouraging results in stove uptake have been reported by many non-governmental organizations, such as Practical Action, Groupe énergies renouvelables, environnement et solidarités (Group for the Environment, Renewable Energy and Solidarity (GERES)) Cambodia and Potential Energy, working in Asia and Africa, and with women centrally involved in stove design, testing and social and conventional marketing (see Global Alliance for Clean Cookstoves, 2013).

The cookstove arena is now firmly enmeshed in the climate mitigation debate. It is routinely asserted that cleaner cookstoves can empower women, improve human health and mitigate global warming, and therefore that there is a win-win nexus of climate, energy and poverty. Reduced solid fuel use reduces harmful emissions, even though all stoves in total produce a very small fraction of total emissions (about 1 to 3 tons of carbon dioxide per year, per stove) (Lee and others, 2013). More critical than the emissions of carbon dioxide may be those of black carbon (soot), an air pollutant, a forcing agent for global warming and a regional climate disruptor, which biomass- and coal-burning stoves produce, and which generates a significant amount of warming in the short-term. In South Asia it is estimated that half of the total emitted black carbon is from biomass-burning stoves, and that it disrupts the monsoons and therefore potentially threatens water availability. It should be noted, however, that detailed research on black carbon sources shows that residential biofuel cooking overall may or may not result in a small warming effect from short-lived pollutants, but the size of the effect, if any, is extremely uncertain. Residential coal burning has a slightly higher short-term warming effect, but again, "with low certainty" (Bond and others, 2013).

The apparent climate impacts have made it possible to finance and market stove programmes through public-private partnerships, the Clean Development Mechanism, the Clean Cooking Loan Fund and other new forms of creative carbon financing.[43] But the data provide little assurance that reducing the burning of biofuel will mitigate near-term climate change in a meaningful way. The so-called co-benefits of climate mitigation from clean stoves, such as better health for, in particular, women, and lower costs for fuel, in terms of the time spent collecting fuel and/or the financial cost, overwhelm the climate benefits. The benefits in terms of women's and children's health and the reduction in their unpaid workloads alone should provide a strong enough rationale for investing in clean cookstoves as part of a sustainable development agenda.

organic carbon (Lam and others, 2012). Not having basic electricity automatically puts a household in the category of "poor" and, by this metric, over 1.3 billion people remain poor.

Though the Millennium Development Goals did not have an electricity (or energy) goal or target, access to basic electricity services is a prerequisite for gender equality and not just for overall development alone (Cabraal, Barnes and Agarwal, 2005). The primary target of Goal 3, on promoting gender equality, was the elimination of gender disparity in education, and access to electricity has allowed more women to read and watch television across all income classes (Pereira and others, 2011, and Energy Sector Management Assistance Program, 2004, cited therein). Small enterprises, often run by women, also need electricity. Access to electricity improves health-care infrastructure

The benefits in terms of women's and children's health and the reduction in their unpaid workloads alone should provide a strong enough rationale for investing in clean cookstoves as part of a sustainable development agenda

4. Electricity

The final example of a transformative investment is electricity. Reliable, safe and affordable lighting transforms lives. Electricity means that men and women can work longer or more flexible hours if needed, that children or adults can study in the evenings with good lighting, and that cell phones, which have become an essential means of communication for the working poor, can be charged. Electric lighting is safer by far than open flame kerosene lamps or candles. Wick-based lighting, such as candles and kerosene lamps, also generates high levels of black carbon, but unlike biomass-burning cookstoves, kerosene lamps emit almost pure black carbon with little

in general because clinics can function after sunset, vaccines can be kept cold and childbirth need not take place in the dark. The maternal mortality ratio in particular is strongly correlated with access to electricity (Sovacool, 2012). Women aged 15 to 34 die in disproportionately high numbers on account of maternal mortality (United Nations, 2013a), and deliveries without light are known to be a significant cause of infections and death. Basic access to electricity is therefore essential for the expansion of women's capabilities.

The cost estimates for bringing modern electricity services to the 1.3 billion people who are currently unserved range widely, but the

Basic access to electricity is essential for the expansion of women's capabilities

World Energy Outlook estimates a need for $49 billion per year until 2030 (International Energy Agency, 2012). The range depends on how capital costs are estimated, but also on what is assumed about fuel prices and appliance efficiencies. Ongoing maintenance costs are usually included for assessing grid electricity costs, but often left out of calculations for smaller home-based or community-based systems. Centralized grid extension remains most efficient for densely populated middle-income urban areas such as in China or South Africa. But capital cost considerations and low prospects for revenue recovery have prevented private sector utilities from entering low-income, sparsely populated, rural markets (Bazilian and others, 2012) even as many developing countries have been pushed, for reasons of efficiency but also of ideology, in the direction of privatizing their energy services.

It is important to consider the current tension between bringing electricity to the unconnected and increasing greenhouse gas emissions, because the conventional model of provision is a centralized grid based on fossil-fuel energy. Overall, the majority of those in the dark are rural residents, and their low capacity to pay, high level of need and global climate change considerations have combined to make decentralized systems based on renewables a leading policy recommendation for sustainable energy, according to Sustainable Energy for All. There are several options within the category of decentralized or microgrid systems using renewable energy. These include extremely small systems averaging around 10W ("pico"), supporting simply a couple of lights and cell-phone charging; or solar home systems, supporting fans, four to five efficient lights and a television, averaging about 30-40W

for commonly sold units; or mini-grid systems which offer several community-scale services, require higher upfront investments, but generate electricity at a lower cost than home systems, as reported by Sustainable Energy for All. Microgrid systems may be faster to scale up and replicate than a centralized grid in low-resource communities, but case studies show that costs and capacity for ongoing maintenance cannot be an afterthought in the cost-benefit analyses. Hybrid renewable-conventional systems are also possible, at the community or multi-community scale, combining photovoltaics with wind, or even with diesel, providing grid-like reliability and a range of productive applications beyond just residential use (Guruswamy, 2011).

Basic electricity access is currently defined as having a connection in the home. Providing a minimal level of electricity to the 1.3 billion people who are currently without access, in order to power basic lighting, a fan and a radio or television, would add up to a tiny fraction of current global electricity consumption, while having potentially transformative effects. Therefore the climate is not in immediate danger from the provision of basic electricity for the poor, even if their entire consumption were to be powered by fossil fuels. But integrating renewables into the grid and expanding decentralized options by using clean power sources that minimize the impact on local health and the level of particulate pollution, are important steps for preventing the lock-down of new fossil-fuel based infrastructures. The provision of basic services is only a start. Poverty eradication will require moving beyond that (Sovacool, 2012). As with the cookstove arena, sustainability in relation to electricity services should reflect the relative effects on climate and on capabilities of both centralized and decentralized, and conventional and renewable, options.

As with all interventions, decentralized rural electrification programmes have succeeded in some areas but failed for financial, political and social reasons in others. And while basic electricity services remain essential for sustainable development, no technology, regardless of its cost, climate resilience, or mode of dissemination can ensure that the electricity generated and used will in fact improve gender equality. Studies on women and electricity have reported that, once there are electric lights, women have more time to be with their children, perform their chores faster and can read more. But for extremely small and limited systems, cooking, studying and television compete for the limited electricity (Jacobson, 2007); intra-household allocation and power will determine who uses the watts and for which purposes (see Agarwal, 1997). It may be that, higher costs notwithstanding, systems with a higher capacity than "pico" will be needed in order for electricity services to actively promote gender equality. Based on the capability enhancement criteria suggested in this chapter, therefore, small, but not pico, systems may turn out to be on the more sustainable path.

D/ INSTITUTIONAL CONTEXT OF INVESTMENTS

The institutional context of investing in sustainability and capabilities is undeniably crucial. Each of the four priority sectors identified depends on innovative and/or affordable technologies, and technologies can easily be seen as the central ingredient for making investments in water, sanitation, cookstoves and electricity a success. But technology is only a part of any investment story, as technologies are disseminated in an institutional and financial context, to users with their own values and views, and within specific political economies. The institutional context significantly determines who has access and on what terms. Many projects in water, sanitation and energy now engage women at every level, from design to marketing to finance. This is particularly true for the more market-based interventions, such as clean cookstoves or off-grid efficient lighting; it is also increasingly the case for water or sanitation systems. But the institutional demands of going to scale for the 1.3 billion people without electricity or the 2.5 billion people without sanitation are truly daunting.

Water, sanitation and electricity have historically gone to scale through public sector investments, as networked utilities have traditionally been monopolies. Since the 1980s, these services in developing countries have opened up to the private sector. Private sector participation increased because the public sector did not provide services to the low-income public and because the global political economy became more market-friendly and more sceptical of the state (see e.g., World Bank, 2003). Over the same period, civil society actors and decentralization became mainstream in these service sectors. The cookstove sector was never fully in the public domain. Stoves have mainly been seen as stand-alone consumer items, despite long-standing (and now increasing) national and donor programmes for improved stoves and biogas-based energy.

The resulting public-private partnerships in the centralized or semi-centralized utilities for developing countries have had mixed results (Bazilian and others, 2011). The literature in support of public-private partnerships has often argued that such partnerships are the only way forward, as the state sector has neither the funds nor the capacity and credibility to expand provision. However, a recent comprehensive study of water and sanitation financing in 17 countries, conducted by the United Nations Inter-agency Mechanism on All Freshwater Related Issues Including Sanitation (UN-Water) and WHO, shows that 80 per cent of the (non-household) funds for this sector continue to come from central, regional and local governments (WHO, 2012). The arguments against public-private partnerships suggest that privatization is reducing the state to a mere upholder of private property and guarantor of private contracts, but overlooks the failure of many states to provide for poor people, and the implications of that failure. The evidence on whether public-private partnerships benefit low-income women, by providing a reliable and efficient service and thus reducing coping costs and uncertainty, or whether they harm women, by requiring monetary contributions and user fees which women may not have, is still mixed.

Though the limitations of government-run programmes have been emphasized in recent decades, and though states are often poorly governed, the evidence suggests that they remain pivotal to social investments at scale. A well-known example is China's rural clean cookstove project; the programme transformed over 100 million households through improved stoves, with a coordinated effort by multiple national ministries, multiple county- and village-level officials, rural energy companies and local energy service enterprises (Sinton and others, 2004). An

The nature of private sector engagement in water, sanitation and energy is rapidly changing, especially for providers working with people in the lowest income quintiles

example of nationally led rural electricity access is the post-apartheid national electrification programme in South Africa. The far-reaching programme was successful in that access to electricity more than doubled within a short time, with selected private sector concessionaires working towards a largely public sector goal.

Such at-scale examples are rare without the state playing a central role. Private enterprise, demand-driven services and finances, bottom-up pressure from non-governmental organizations and the demonstration effects of pilot projects, are all critical. But much of the literature on the importance and innovation of private actors in essential services concludes that the state needs to set and enforce an enabling policy framework, provide direct assistance to the poorest, and direct the flow and targeting of collective goods, if water and energy services are to be universally provided. Different reasons have been suggested for the failure of promising interventions to scale up, such as insufficient state subsidies, weak infrastructure, weak governance and poor regulation (Zhang and Smith, 2007; Bailis and others, 2009; Pereira and others, 2011; Harris, Kooy and Jones, 2011; Sovacool, 2012). Private actors cannot capture spillover benefits, or provide services to an extremely poor user base, or guarantee either basic needs or environmental integrity. This is not their mandate.

At the same time, the nature of private sector engagement in water, sanitation and energy is rapidly changing, especially for providers working with people in the lowest income quintiles. Rather than large corporate entities, they are small-scale, semi-formal entities sometimes purely commercial, at other times social as well as commercial, and mostly agile and entrepreneurial. It is critical that the public sector engages with the private sector(s) in sustainable development efforts, and regulates it while taking advantage of its service-creation and market-creation potential. Yet regulation and oversight is a capacity that smaller states may lack, especially relative to the well-financed corporations with which they sometimes have to negotiate. Regulation and oversight of the private and public sectors, therefore, are also the business of civil society and social movement representatives. These entities, heterogeneous though they may be, are often effective pressure groups and/or watchdogs on behalf of unserved or marginalized communities.

In this complex institutional environment, where different providers are operating side by side, investments for sustainable development can only go to scale with alliances among all the players in the development arena. Contemporary efforts show that such alliances are indeed possible in the water, sanitation and energy sectors. Grameen Shakti is one of the primary private (but non-profit) sector actors in off-grid electricity in Bangladesh and has installed over 1 million home solar systems. It uses financing provided by the International Finance Corporation and the Government of Bangladesh to extend generous microcredit terms to its buyers (Pachauri and others, 2012). The extensive networks of rainwater harvesting systems in India, pioneered by groups such as Tarun Bharat Sangh and Gravis, are now going to scale with government support, in some cases government mandates, after hundreds of successful demonstrations (India, Ministry of Water Resources, 2012). Community-led total

sanitation, a subsidy-free participatory approach to latrine building and use, is expanding rapidly in sub-Saharan Africa with the support of international agencies and national governments (e.g., Rukuni, 2010). Cookstove projects with women's groups, community groups, social enterprises and for-profit stove makers are working with millions of customers in Africa, Central America and South and South-East Asia. These examples are proof that transformative alliances can and do exist, and that new forms of state-business-society ties can enable gender-responsive sustainable development.

Despite the shortcoming of many state-run efforts, the historical evidence points to the need for states to enter into contracts with their people, and to honour those contracts, at least in part. It is akin to what has been called the "developmental state", in which the state, in concert with other social actors, is ultimately accountable to all women and men (Evans, 1995). It is compatible with the call for countries to realize their commitments to human rights, which include gender equality and an adequate standard of living. Sustainable and capability-expanding development, at scale, needs an active and accountable state.

E/ FINANCING INVESTMENTS FOR SUSTAINABLE DEVELOPMENT

Financing pro-poor gender-responsive investment in sustainable water, sanitation and energy services is a formidable proposition, especially for countries with low per-capita GDP. The difficulty of financing such

investments to scale must be acknowledged and budgetary competition with other sectors, including health, defence, education, debt repayment and agriculture, must also be faced. Financing investments for the lowest quintiles requires an enabling environment in developed and developing countries alike. The following list is by no means exhaustive, but serves to show that both traditional and non-traditional sources of financing for water, sanitation and energy services exist and can be usefully harnessed and redirected towards sustainability and gender equality:

(a) Central government domestic resource mobilization (e.g., progressive taxation on income, including the corporate sector) is central to any new social contract that is pro-poor and responsive to gender equality;

(b) Local and municipal government financing;

(c) Public financing of infrastructure, with central or local government oversight and monitoring, but with the provision or supply either contracted out, or provided through market forces;

(d) Redirecting international development lending away from a large-infrastructure bias;

(e) Bond and portfolio equity financing (increasingly common for large infrastructure, allowing for funds to be raised nationally or internationally);

(f) Community-driven development financing or social funds (these may be of limited scalability);

(g) Developed countries meeting the target of 0.7 per cent of their gross national product being apportioned for official development assistance to developing countries (and ring-fencing priority sectors such as water and sanitation within that 0.7%);

(h) Mobilize resources through a tax on global financial transactions;

(i) Reducing the many existing, and often legal, avenues of tax evasion;

(j) Removal of fossil fuel subsidies in the Group of 20 (G20) and in the newly industrializing countries;

(k) Redirecting military budgets;

(l) Reducing trade-distorting agricultural subsidies and exports in developed countries, which make it difficult for farmers in poor countries to compete, as pointed out in chapter 4;

(m) Climate financing in accordance with the obligations of the United Nations Framework Convention on Climate Change, to be channelled in part through the Green Climate Fund;

(n) Other smaller but potentially pivotal funding categories, such as adaptation and mitigation financing including the United Nations Collaborative Programme on Reducing Emissions from Deforestation and Forest Degradation in Developing Countries and related processes (REDD and REDD+), green microfinance and possibly future carbon taxes (bearing in mind that such instruments are important but imperfect, and may be no more pro-poor or gender-responsive than traditional government financing).

Both traditional and non-traditional sources of financing for water, sanitation and energy services exist and can be usefully harnessed and redirected towards sustainability and gender equality

Multiple actors have a role in implementing and monitoring such financing regimes, including governments, multilateral lenders, regional development banks, United Nations entities, traditional development assistance institutions and the private sector. With the growth of public-private partnerships and increasing involvement of the private sector in development, stronger accountability frameworks are needed to ensure compliance with human rights standards, particularly as public money is often used to draw in (or "top up") private investments. It is important to highlight the role of grants versus the role of

loans for community-based water, sanitation and clean energy, and for adaptation measures more broadly. Lending requires poor countries and possibly poor communities to repay the loans. When these repayments result in shrinking social sector spending, more unpaid work for women may ensue. The criteria laid out in this chapter indicate that such financing is not appropriate for sustainable development.

In sum, for sustainable development to be compatible with internationally accepted human rights norms, gender equality is a necessary

Taking turns at the tap in Maane
Dobhaan, Nepal, 2013

transformative for women's and girls' health and dignity, especially for those from poorer households. For this to happen, investments cannot be designed in a gender-neutral way but need to take the specific needs of women and girls into account, including the circumstances under which they study, work and live.

Investments in the four selected domains are, in effect, investments in the determinants of health and opportunity. It is crucial to choose practical, selective and relevant indicators, such as the reduction of unpaid care work, in order to assess the impact of these specific investments on the capabilities of women and girls. Additional metrics of assessment may also be chosen, such as water quality or carbon emissions or pro-poor income growth, or similar measures relevant to a specific societal investment. However, the approach for such investments does question a carbon-first-and-foremost approach to water, sanitation and energy for the poor without due attention to other dimensions of sustainable development.

It is important to recognize that effective investments at scale are difficult and uncertain and depend on gender-sensitive and context-sensitive design as well as financing (Schalatek, 2012). Moreover, such investments call for transformative alliances between policymakers, donors, the state and the private and civil sectors. Investments at scale (whether sustainable or otherwise) need the reach and organizing power of the state; and the state needs the mobilizing power and vigilance of collective action and social movements to ensure it honour its contracts. Sustainable development can be pioneered, demonstrated and encouraged, but ultimately not spearheaded, by non-governmental organizations, donors and the private sector. Basic but transformative investing needs much more than innovative technologies and innovative financing to be sustainable. Moreover, it must be underpinned by the agency and leadership of women and girls taking the decisions that are so critical for their lives, livelihoods and communities in the pursuit of sustainable development.

component of any chosen pathway(s). Investments towards socially transformative development should consider women's capability enhancement, especially at the lowest quintile, as a non-negotiable goal. This means that sustainable development efforts, globally or regionally, must be directed towards key sectors from which poor women are the main beneficiaries. Against this backdrop, water, sanitation, cookstoves and electricity were identified as priority areas for investments that can promote gender-responsive sustainable development. Each of these sectors could be

CHAPTER /7

CONCLUSIONS AND POLICY RECOMMENDATIONS

The present *World Survey* has examined the important links between gender equality and sustainability. The *World Survey* is published at a crucial moment, at a time when the international community has recognized that dominant patterns of development and growth are unsustainable in economic, social and environmental terms and is defining the future sustainable development agenda. The Open Working Group of the General Assembly on Sustainable Development Goals, the establishment of which was mandated in the outcome document of the United Nations Conference on Sustainable Development, has since worked on a proposal for future sustainable development goals. The vital importance of gender equality and the empowerment of women as a core part of the post-2015 development agenda has been a strong and recurring theme in the discussions of the Open Working Group.

Current trends in relation to growth, employment, food, population, water and sanitation, and energy provide examples of how unsustainable development and gender inequality reinforce each other. Economic growth trajectories continue to perpetuate gender inequalities, confining women to low-paid jobs and relying on women's unpaid care work, while at the same time exploiting natural resources and damaging ecosystems and biodiversity. The focus of food policy on aggregate production has not only neglected pressing challenges posed by climate change, but also issues of access to and the right to food for all, along with the complex gendered dynamics of local and global food markets, intra-household allocation of food and production systems that drive hunger and malnutrition. Narrowly focused population policies may prescribe coercive measures to achieve fertility reduction that can have significant implications for women's enjoyment of human rights. Further, the dominant population paradigm shifts attention away from patterns of consumption and production, which play a more significant role than population in environmental degradation. The lack of universal access to water,

sanitation and energy that are environmentally sustainable and of good quality bears significant consequences for women's and girls' human rights and capabilities.

Power imbalances in gender relations, in the exercise of rights, access to and control of resources, and participation in decision-making, persist as a significant obstacle to women's full and equal contribution to and opportunity to benefit from sustainable development. Looking forward to the post-2015 development agenda, efforts to achieve gender equality and sustainable development should be grounded in human rights and underpinned by principles of equality and justice for present and future generations. As such, sustainable development is economic, social and environmental development that ensures human well-being and dignity, ecological integrity, gender equality and social justice, now and in the future.

All sustainable development policies and frameworks, at the global, regional, national and local levels, must include an explicit commitment to gender equality and the realization of women's and girls' human rights and capabilities. This requires redressing gender inequality, discrimination and disadvantage and addressing their intersection with other inequalities. Women's collective action and full and equal participation in all aspects of decision-making related to policy development and monitoring must be supported and are central for achieving results.

Addressing sustainable development and gender equality together is vital for harnessing the synergies between both objectives. Gender equality can have a catalytic effect on achieving sustainable development. Acknowledging women's knowledge, agency and collective action offers the potential to improve resource productivity and efficiency; to enhance ecosystem conservation and sustainable use; and to build more sustainable, low-carbon and climate-resilient food, energy, water and sanitation, and health systems. Women have been and must continue to be central actors in promoting sustainability and green transformations. However, approaches that draw on women's knowledge and time without conferring upon women the rights and the benefits of sustainable development can further reinforce gender stereotypes and entrench gender inequalities.

Achieving sustainable development means reconciling economic, social and environmental concerns and objectives. There are always tensions and trade-offs to negotiate and harmonize. Some pathways promote environmental sustainability without taking sufficiently into account gender equality, and others promote gender equality and neglect key dimensions of sustainability. Any development pathway will only be sustainable if it enhances women's capabilities, respects and protects their rights and reduces and redistributes their unpaid care work.

The negotiation of policy dilemmas to achieve sustainable development and gender equality requires inclusive learning and deliberation processes and ways to monitor exclusions, trade-offs and unexpected opportunities. The active participation, leadership and creativity of women, civil society and women's organizations, communities and all concerned individuals in such processes are critical.

Renewed social contracts between states and all people are needed, where states fulfil their obligations as the duty bearers and rights holders claim and enjoy rights.

States play central roles in delivering on commitments to gender equality, setting standards and regulations for resource use and providing public services and investments for sustainable development

States play central roles in delivering on commitments to gender equality, setting standards and regulations for resource use and providing public services and investments for sustainable development. Public investment is necessary for scaling-up key innovations for gender-responsive public goods, such as the provision of water supplies, appropriate sanitation facilities and modern energy services. Alliances between the state, private sector and civil society actors that advance gender equality and sustainable development also have a vital role to play. In particular, voices and movements from the margins that offer powerful alternatives for transformed, more sustainable futures grounded in gender equality and human rights should be sought, heard and acted upon.

The *World Survey* proposes three criteria to assess whether sustainable development is in line with gender equality and women's human rights: first, compliance with human rights standards and the realization of women's capabilities; second, attention to the unpaid care work of women and girls, especially those in poor and marginalized households and communities; and third, full and equal participation by women and girls in all aspects of sustainable development.

In order to ensure that efforts to achieve sustainable development meet the criteria, Member States should fully implement the commitment to gender equality and the empowerment of women contained in the Beijing Platform for Action and the outcome of the twenty-third special session of the General Assembly. States parties to the Convention on the Elimination of All Forms of Discrimination against Women should fully implement their obligations under the Convention.

To that end, States, international organizations, including the United Nations, and human rights mechanisms, the private sector, non-governmental organizations, trade unions and other stakeholders may wish to take the following actions:

(a) On sustainable development and gender equality overall:

(i) Develop and implement policies on the economic, social and environmental dimensions of sustainable development in line with international norms and standards on gender equality, non-discrimination and human rights;

(ii) Promote transitions to sustainable low-carbon, climate-resilient consumption and production patterns while ensuring gender equality;

(iii) Ensure women's right to an adequate standard of living, through increasing access to decent work and providing gender-responsive, universally accessible and high quality services, social protection measures and infrastructure, including education, health, water and sanitation, and energy;

(iv) Promote a renewed social contract between states and people that ensures the financing and implementation of sustainable development, with universal access to public goods and services and common pool resources, particularly for the poorest groups of women and girls;

(v) Recognize, reduce and redistribute unpaid care work between women and men within households, and between households and the state by expanding basic services and infrastructure that are accessible to all;

(vi) Respect, protect and promote sexual and reproductive health and rights for all, particularly women and girls, across the life cycle;

(vii) Protect the commons and prevent the appropriation and exploitation of natural resources by private and public interests, through state oversight and multi-stakeholder regulation;

(viii) Ensure the full and equal participation of women and girls in sustainable development policies and initiatives as actors, leaders and decision makers;

(b) Green economy, gender equality and care:

(ix) Ensure that macroeconomic policies are geared towards creating decent work and sustainable livelihoods and reducing inequalities based on gender, age, income, geographical location and other context-specific characteristics;

(x) Prioritize the development of gender-responsive policies aimed at generating decent work, with a focus on labour market segregation, gender wage gaps and the unequal distribution of unpaid care work within households, and between households and the state;

(xi) Ensure that green growth strategies are gender-responsive and socially, economically and environmentally sustainable;

(xii) Ensure that green growth policies increase access for women, particularly for poor and marginalized women, to high quality jobs in sustainable and low-carbon industries;

(xiii) Invest in women's skills development and education to increase their access to green jobs, including targeted measures to increased women's education, employment and leadership in science, technology, engineering and mathematics;

(xiv) Transform service and informal sector work, including paid care work, into sources of sustainable livelihoods and decent employment through specific policies and regulations that are aligned with decent work standards;

(xv) Promote and protect the rights of domestic workers by ratifying the Domestic Workers Convention, 2011 (No. 189) of the International Labour Organization and by developing and implementing labour market and employment policies to guarantee decent pay and conditions for domestic work;

(c) Food security:

(xvi) Develop and advance global standards and norms to support food security and women and men smallholder farmers in areas such as equitable trade rules, regulation of commodity markets and large-scale land investments, including for biofuels;

(xvii) Design and implement comprehensive gender-responsive and human rights-based policies that ensure equitable and sustainable access to adequate, safe, affordable and nutritious food for all, addressing the specific constraints individuals and households face in acquiring food through own production, wage exchange and social transfers;

(xviii) Guarantee food security for all by provisioning of high quality through public food reserves, food subsidies and/or school feeding programmes, among others, to ease the pressure on food-insecure households and reduce gender bias in the intra-household allocation of food;

(xix) Work to eradicate discriminatory attitudes and behaviours, especially with regard to women's and girls' right to food and the intra-household distribution of food through concrete and long-term measures;

(xx) Increase agricultural and food system resilience to climate change, drawing on the knowledge of farmers, particularly women smallholders, and facilitating the exchange of knowledge and good practices in crop and land management to mitigate and adapt to climate and environmental stresses;

(xxi) Address the institutional constraints that women smallholder farmers face, such as removing gender discrimination in laws, policies and practice in access to land, common property resources, credit, inputs, machinery and livestock, financial and extension services, with specific attention to marginalized groups of women, by providing price supports and prioritizing public procurement from women smallholder farmers;

(xxii) Promote decent work and adequate wages for agricultural and informal workers, especially women, through labour market regulation and employment policies that guarantee decent employment conditions for all and prevent discrimination against women;

(d) Population:

(xxiii) Ground sustainable population policies in sexual and reproductive health and rights, including the provision of universally accessible quality sexual and reproductive health services, information and education across the life cycle, including safe and effective methods of modern contraception, maternal health care, comprehensive sexuality education and safe abortion;

(xxiv) Ensure that health services are available, accessible, acceptable and of appropriate quality for all women and girls;

(xxv) Design and implement population policies to address the full range of measures related to women's fertility, including measures to increase access to high quality education and access to decent work;

(xxvi) Ensure women's participation and voice in decision-making at all levels regarding population and sustainable development;

(e) Investments that accelerate the realization of gender equality:

(xxvii) Assess investments in services and infrastructure in terms of the gender-specific costs, benefits and risks they present for the realization of women's and girls' rights and capabilities, with particular focus on the poorest groups;

(xxviii) Prioritize investments to ensure universal access to water, with specific attention to distance, quality, affordability and the ways in which women use water, with a view to reducing unpaid care work;

(xxix) Ensure access to clean, private and safe sanitation for all women and girls that is responsive to gender-specific needs such as menstrual hygiene and addressing the risk of violence in accessing sanitation facilities;

(xxx) Invest at scale in efficient solid-fuel stoves or cooking technologies that use cleaner fuels, especially in rural and peri-urban areas, and encourage stove uptake by involving women in stove design, testing and social marketing;

(xxxi) Invest at scale in initiatives to provide basic and affordable electricity access to unserved and underserved populations, particularly rural populations, with a view to enabling health-care facilities to function; supporting income generation and educational attainment; and reducing women's unpaid care work, enabling them to enjoy leisure time;

(xxxii) Ensure women's full and equal participation and leadership in decision-making processes at all levels to determine investment in and usage of water, sanitation and energy technologies at the household, local, national, regional and global levels;

(xxxiii) Develop public–private–civil sector alliances that enable investments at scale to guarantee universal access to essential services and infrastructure, while ensuring compliance with human rights standards;

(f) Financing measures:

(xxxiv) Increase financial resources for sustainable development and gender equality through: developed countries meeting target of 0.7 per cent of their gross national product apportioned for official development assistance to developing countries; introducing a tax on financial transactions; reducing existing avenues of tax evasion; members of the Group of 20 and newly industrializing countries removing fossil fuel subsidies; and reducing trade-distorting agricultural subsidies and exports in developed countries;

(xxxv) Mobilize domestic resources for sustainable development and gender equality through progressive taxation on income and corporate sector profits, addressing tax evasion and illicit financial flows, and redirecting military budgets;

(xxxvi) Create an enabling environment in developed and developing countries for financing green, pro-poor and gender-responsive investments at the national and international levels;

(g) Data and statistics:

(xxxvii) Improve the systematic collection, dissemination and analysis of gender statistics and of data and information disaggregated by sex and age, through financial and technical support and capacity-building, on the participation of women in household decision-making, the role of women in food production and management, women's access to land and other resources, and time-use and unpaid care work;

(xxxviii) Ensure the collection, analysis and use of accurate and complete data disaggregated by sex and age at the individual and household levels on food and nutrition security, including hunger and malnutrition, and on resilience and adaptation to climate change;

(xxxix) Collect and disseminate statistics regularly and report on the minimum set of gender indicators agreed by the Statistical Commission;

(xl) Develop international standards and methodologies to improve data on unpaid care work, women's participation at all levels of decision-making and women's ownership and control of assets and productive resources.

ENDNOTES

1. Report of the United Nations Conference on Environment and Development, Rio de Janeiro, 3-14 June 1992, vol. I, Resolutions Adopted by the Conference (United Nations publication, Sales No. E.93.I.8 and corrigendum), resolution 1, annex I.

2. Report of the Fourth World Conference on Women, Beijing, 4-15 September 1995 (United Nations publication, Sales No. E.96.IV.13), chap. I, resolution 1, annexes I and II.

3. See http://huairou.org/south-asian-network-grassroots-womens-leaders-community-resilience-formally-launched-kathmandu-nepal (accessed 26 June 2014).

4. Public goods are recognized as having benefits that cannot be easily confined to a single "buyer" or user of that good; the benefits of a public good spill over to others. They are goods which people consume together rather than separately, such as a malaria-free environment, clean air, education, sanitation, and so on.

5. United Nations, Treaty Series, vol. 1249, No. 20378.

6. United Nations, Treaty Series, vol. 1771, No. 30822.

7. United Nations, Treaty Series, vol. 1760, No. 30619.

8. United Nations, Treaty Series, vol. 1954, No. 33480.

9. Report of the International Conference on Population and Development, Cairo, 5-13 September 1994 (United Nations publication, Sales No. E.95.XIII.18), chap. I, resolution 1, annex.

10. Report of the World Food Summit, 13-17 November 1996 (WFS 96/REP), part one, appendix.

11. See also World Survey on the Role of Women in Development: Globalization, Gender and Work (United Nations publication, Sales No. E.99.IV.8).

12. "States shall cooperate in a spirit of global partnership to conserve, protect and restore the health and integrity of the Earth's ecosystem. In view of the different contributions to global environmental degradation, States have common but differentiated responsibilities. The developed countries acknowledge the responsibility that they bear in the international pursuit to sustainable development in view of the pressures their societies place on the global environment and of the technologies and financial resources they command." See principle 7, Report of the United Nations Conference on Environment and Development, Rio de Janeiro, 3-14 June 1992, vol. I, Resolutions Adopted by the Conference (United Nations publication, Sales No. E.93.I.8 and corrigendum), resolution 1, annex I.

13. See, for example, http://nupge.ca/content/%5Bnid%5D/economy-or-environment-its-false-choice.

14. For more information, see http://viacampesina.org/en/index.php/main-issues-mainmenu-27/ women-mainmenu-39/1549-chile-women-farmers-to-teach-the-region-agroecology (accessed 26 June 2014).

15. Employment that is not covered or insufficiently covered by formal arrangements, including lack of protection in the event of non-payment of wages, compulsory overtime or extra shifts, lay-offs without notice or compensation, unsafe working conditions and the absence of social benefits such as pensions, pay for sick leave and health insurance.

16. See also World Survey on the Role of Women in Development: Women's Control over Economic Resources and Access to Financial Resources, including Microfinance (United Nations publication, Sales No. E.09.IV.7).

17. Macroeconomic policy refers to interventions by governments and central banks that affect conditions throughout the entire economy through their impact on aggregate income, total expenditure, investment, credit, interest rates, exchange rates and capital flows, among other factors. Macroeconomic policies are usually divided into fiscal policies (government spending and taxation) and monetary policies which influence the money supply and the availability of credit. Other policy areas, such as trade and financial market policies, can also have economy-wide effects.

18. Financialization goes beyond the proliferation of financial markets and the corresponding speculative activity, to refer to the extension of those markets to an ever-expanding range of activities and sectors, such as pensions, health care, housing and so forth (Fine, 2012).

19. Global imbalances refer to the distribution of large current account deficits and surpluses across a number of countries.

20. Decent work includes high quality employment generation; workers' rights, including freedom from discrimination; access to social protection; and ongoing social dialogue among a variety of economic and civil society organizations (ILO, 2012).

21. See www.ilo.org/global/research/global-reports/global-employment-trends/WCMS_195447/lang--en/index.htm.

22. See Waste Pickers, 2014, Women in Informal Employment: Globalizing and Organizing, information available from http://wiego.org/informal-economy/occupational-groups/waste-pickers (accessed 24 January 2014).

23. Definitions and usage of social security and social protection vary widely, across both disciplines and international organizations. The World Survey draws on the approach of ILO (2014) to use both terms

interchangeably as referring to measures that secure protection against, inter alia: lack of work-related income (or insufficient income) caused by sickness, disability, maternity, employment injury, unemployment, old age, or death of a family member; lack of access or unaffordable access to health care; insufficient family support, particularly for children and adult dependants; general poverty and social exclusion.

24. The phrase appears to have originated from the report of the Special Rapporteur on the right to food (E/CN.4/Sub.2/1987/23).

25. See E/2000/22 and Corr.1, annex I, General Comment No. 13; E/2001/22, annex IV, General Comment No. 14; E/2003/22, annex IV, General Comment No. 15; E/2006/22, annex C, General Comment No. 18; and E/2008/22, annex VII, General Comment No. 19.

26. Paid care work includes occupations in which workers are supposed to provide a face-to-face service that develops the human capabilities of the recipient. "Human capabilities" refer to health, skills or proclivities that are useful to oneself or others. These include physical and mental health, physical skills, cognitive skills and emotional skills, such as self-discipline, empathy and care. Examples of caring labour include the work of teachers, nurses, childcare workers and therapists (England, Budig and Folbre 2002).

27. Two important exceptions are the models presented in Braunstein, van Staveren and Tavani (2011) and Seguino (2010).

28. Defined as the proportion of the population that does not meet a minimum level of dietary energy consumption. This indicator measures food insecurity at the national level and is defined by the Food and Agriculture Organization of the United Nations.

29. See United Nations Children's Fund (UNICEF) Childinfo, available from http://data.unicef.org/nutrition/malnutrition (accessed 8 May 2014).

30. See, for example, Fatima Shabodien, "Women farm workers dying for food", Oxfam online discussion essay series on making the food system work for women (2012), available from http://blogs.oxfam.org/en/blogs/women-farm-workers-dying-food (accessed on 18 July 2014).

31. The food production index set at 100 for 2004-2006 was 118.0 in 2012, against 75.3 in 1994.

32. Report of the Fourth World Conference on Women, Beijing, 4-15 September 1995 (United Nations publication, Sales No. E.96.IV.13), chap. IV, resolution 1, annex II, paras. 96 and 97.

33. The average number of children a hypothetical cohort of women would have at the end of their reproductive period if they were subject during their whole lives to the fertility rates of a given period and if they were not subject to mortality. It is expressed as children per woman (United Nations, 2013c).

34. See United Nations, Department of Economic and Social Affairs, Population Division, Population Estimates and Projections Section, http://esa.un.org/unpd/wpp/Excel-Data/ fertility.htm (accessed 16 June 2014).

35. "The lack of balance between birth and death rates is particularly pronounced in many developing countries experiencing population momentum. This phenomenon occurs when a large proportion of a country's population is of childbearing age. Even if the fertility rate of people in developing countries reaches replacement level, that is if couples have only enough children to replace themselves when they die, for several decades the absolute numbers of people being born still will exceed the numbers of people dying", see www.worldbank.org/ depweb/english/modules/social/pgr/index02.html (accessed 22 June 2014).

36. "Excess female deaths in a given year represent women who would not have died in the previous year if they had lived in a high-income country, after accounting for the overall health environment of the country they live in" (World Bank, 2012).

37. See the essay by Sen (1990). Missing women refers to the excess mortality of girls and women in a given country compared to areas of the world where women/girls and men/boys receive the same level of care.

38. United Nations Development Programme, Human Development Report, Human Development Index, http://hdr.undp.org/en/statistics/hdi (accessed on 27 June 2014).

39. The minimum set of gender indicators adopted by the Statistical Commission in 2013 provides a guide for the national production and international compilation of gender statistics. See Department of Economic and Social Affairs, Statistics Division, Gender Statistics, available from http://unstats.un.org/unsd/gender/default.html (accessed 16 July 2014).

40. The Joint Monitoring Programme on Water Supply and Sanitation of the World Health Organization (WHO) and UNICEF is the United Nations mechanism for monitoring regional and national progress in access to water and sanitation. It uses globally and nationally supported household surveys as its primary data source, and is considered the most comprehensive data set tracking water and sanitation globally.

41. More information available from http://water.org/.

42. More information available from http://saner.gy/.

43. More information available from the website of the Global Alliance for Clean Cookstoves, http://carbonfinanceforcookstoves.org.

REFERENCES*

Abe, A. (2010). The changing shape of the care diamond: the case of child and elderly care in Japan. Gender and Development Programme Paper, No. 9. Geneva: United Nations Research Institute for Social Development.

Adams, V., M. Murphy and A. E. Clarke (2009). Anticipation: technoscience, life, affect, temporality. *Subjectivity*, vol. 28, No. 1, pp. 246–265.

Adams, W. M. (2004). *Against Extinction: The Story of Conservation*. London: Earthscan.

Agarwal, B. (1992). The gender and environment debate: lessons from India. *Feminist Studies*, vol. 18, No. 1, pp. 119–158.

—— (1997). Environmental action, gender equity and women's participation. *Development and Change*, vol. 28, No. 1, pp. 1–44.

—— (2002). Gender inequality, cooperation and environmental sustainability. SFI working paper. Santa Fe, New Mexico: Santa Fe Institute.

—— (2010). *Gender and Green Governance: The Political Economy of Women's Presence Within and Beyond Community Forestry*. Oxford: Oxford University Press.

—— (2012). Food security, productivity, and gender inequality. IEG Working Paper, No. 320. New Delhi: Institute of Economic Growth.

—— (2014). Food sovereignty, food security and democratic choice: critical contradictions, difficult conciliations. *Journal of Peasant Studies*. (Published online).

Anand, S., and A. Sen (2000). Human development and economic sustainability. *World Development*, vol. 28, No. 12, pp. 2029–2049.

Anenberg, S. C., and others (2013). Cleaner cooking solutions to achieve health, climate and economic cobenefits. *Environmental Science and Technology*, vol. 47, No. 9, pp. 3944–3952.

Antonopoulos, R., and I. Hirway, eds. (2010). *Unpaid Work and the Economy: Gender, Time Use and Poverty in Developing Countries*. New York: Palgrave Macmillan.

Arza, C. (2014). The gender dimensions of pension systems. Background paper prepared for the United Nations Entity for Gender Equality and the Empowerment of Women. New York.

Bailis, R., and others (2009). Arresting the killer in the kitchen: the promises and pitfalls of commercializing improved cookstoves. *World Development*, vol. 37, No. 10, pp. 1694–1705.

Bain, C. (2010). Structuring the flexible and feminized labor market: GlobalGAP standards for agricultural labor in Chile. *Signs: Journal of Women in Culture and Society*, vol. 35, No. 2, pp. 343–370.

Barrientos, S., and B. Evers (2014). Gendered production networks: push and pull on corporate responsibility? In *New Frontiers in Feminist Political Economy*, S. M. Rai and G. Waylen, eds. New York: Routledge.

Baum, R., J. Luh and J. Bartram (2013). Sanitation: a global estimate of sewerage connections without treatment and the resulting impact on MDG progress. *Environmental Science and Technology*, vol. 47, No. 4, pp. 1994–2000.

Bazilian, M., and others (2011). Interactions between energy security and climate change: a focus on developing countries. *Energy Policy*, vol. 39, No. 6, pp. 3750–3756.

Bazilian, M., and others (2012). Energy access scenarios to 2030 for the power sector in sub-Saharan Africa. *Utilities Policy*, vol. 20, No. 1, pp. 1–16.

Benería, L., and M. Roldán (1987). *The Crossroads of Class and Gender: Industrial Homework, Subcontracting, and Household Dynamics in Mexico City*. Chicago: University of Chicago Press.

Bernanke, B. S. (2011). Global imbalances: links to economic and financial stability. Statement to the Banque de France Financial Stability Review Launch Event. Paris, 18 February.

Black, M., and G. Fawcett (2008). *The Last Taboo: Opening the Door on the Global Sanitation Crisis*. London: Earthscan.

Blecker, R. (2012). Global imbalances and the U.S. trade deficit. In *After the Great Recession: The Struggle for Economic Recovery and Growth*, B. Cynamon, S. Fazzari and M. Setterfield, eds. New York: Cambridge University Press.

* Symbols of United Nations documents are composed of capital letters combined with figures.

Blecker, R. A., and S. Seguino (2002). Macroeconomic effects of reducing gender wage inequality in an export-oriented, semi-industrialized economy. *Review of Development Economics*, vol. 6, No. 1, pp. 103-119.

Blumberg, R. (1991). Income under female versus male control: hypotheses from a theory of gender stratification and data from the third world. In *Gender, Family and Economy: The Triple Overlap*, R. Blumberg, ed. Newbury Park, California: Sage.

Bond, T. C., and others (2013). Bounding the role of black carbon in the climate system: a scientific assessment. *Journal of Geophysical Research: Atmospheres*, vol. 118, No. 11, pp. 5380-5552.

Borras, S. M., Jr. (2004). La vía campesina: an evolving transnational social movement. TNI Briefing Series, No. 2004/6. Amsterdam: Transnational Institute.

Borras, S. M., Jr., and others (2011). Towards a better understanding of global land grabbing: an editorial introduction. *Journal of Peasant Studies*, vol. 38, No. 2, pp. 209-216.

Boyce, J. K. (2011). The environment as our common heritage. Acceptance speech for the Fair Sharing of the Common Heritage Award of the Media Freedom Foundation and Project Censored. 8 February.

Boyce, J. K., S. Narain and E. A. Stanton, eds. (2007). *Reclaiming Nature: Environmental Justice and Ecological Restoration*. London: Anthem Press.

Boyce, J. K., and M. Riddle (2007). Cap and dividend: how to curb global warming while protecting the incomes of American families. Working Paper, No. 150. Amherst, Massachusetts: Political Economy Research Institute.

Braunstein, E. (2013). Economic growth and social reproduction: gender inequality as cause and consequence. Background paper prepared for United Nations Entity for Gender Equality and the Empowerment of Women (UN-Women). New York.

Braunstein, E., I. van Staveren and D. Tavani (2011). Embedding care and unpaid work in macroeconomic modeling: a structuralist approach. *Feminist Economics*, vol. 17, No. 4, pp. 5-31.

Braunstein, E., and J. Heintz (2008). Gender bias and central bank policy: employment and inflation reduction. *International Review of Applied Economics*, vol. 22, No. 2, pp. 173-186.

Braunstein, E., and M. Brenner (2007). Foreign direct investment and gendered wages in urban China. *Feminist Economics*, vol. 13, Nos. 3-4, pp. 213-237.

Buckingham-Hatfield, S. (2002). Gender equality: a prerequisite for sustainable development. *Geography*, vol. 87, No. 3, pp. 227-233.

Budig, M., and J. Misra (2010). How care-work employment shapes earnings in cross-national perspective. *International Labour Review*, vol. 149, No. 4, pp. 441-460.

Budlender, D. (2010). What do time use studies tell us about unpaid care work? Evidence from seven countries. In *Time Use Studies and Unpaid Care Work*, D. Budlender, ed. New York: Routledge.

Cabraal, R. A., D. F. Barnes and S. G. Agarwal (2005). Productive uses of energy for rural development. *Annual Review of Environment and Resources*, vol. 30, pp. 117-144.

Carson, R. (1962). *Silent Spring*. Boston: Houghton Mifflin.

Cecelski, E. (1984). *The Rural Energy Crisis, Women's Work and Family Welfare: Perspectives and Approaches to Action*. World Employment Programme Research Working Paper, WEP 10/WP.35. Geneva: International Labour Organization.

Cela, B., I. Dankelman, and J. Stern, eds. (2013). *Powerful Synergies: Gender Equality, Economic Development and Environmental Sustainability*. New York: United Nations Development Programme.

Chai, J., I. Ortiz and X. Sire (2010). Protecting salaries of frontline teachers and health workers. Working Brief. United Nations Children's Fund.

Chan, C. K-C., and M. Ching Lam (2012). The reality and challenges of green jobs in China: an exploration. *International Journal of Labour Research*, vol. 4, No. 2, pp. 189-207.

Chattopadhyay, R., and E. Duflo (2004). Women as policy makers: evidence from a randomized policy experiment in India. *Econometrica*, vol. 72, No. 5, pp. 1409-1443.

Chen, M., and others (2005). *Progress of the World's Women 2005: Women, Work and Poverty*. New York: United Nations Development Fund for Women.

Coleman-Jensen, A., M. Nord and A. Singh (2013). *Household Food Security in the United States in 2012*. Economic Research Report No. 155. Washington, D.C.: United States Department of Agriculture.

Connelly, M. (2008). *Fatal Misconception: The Struggle to Control World Population*. Cambridge, Massachusetts: Harvard University Press.

Secretariat of the Convention on Biodiversity and Women's Environment and Development Organization (2012). Gender equality and the Convention on Biological Diversity: a compilation of decision text.

Corbera, E., and H. Schroeder (2010). Governing and implementing REDD+. *Environmental Science and Policy*, vol. 14, No. 2, pp. 89-99.

Corbera, E., and K. Brown (2008). Building institutions to trade ecosystem services: marketing forest carbon in Mexico. *World Development*, vol. 36, No. 10, pp. 1956-1979.

Cripps, F., A. Izurieta and A. Singh (2011). Global imbalances, under-consumption and over-borrowing: the state of the world economy and future policies. *Development and Change*, vol. 42, No. 1, pp. 228-261.

Crola, J. D. (2011). Preparing for thin cows: why the G20 should keep buffer stocks on the agenda. Oxfam Briefing Note. Oxford: Oxfam International.

Dankelman, I., and J. Davidson (1988). *Women and the Environment in the Third World: Alliance for the Future*. London: Earthscan.

De Benoist, B., and others, eds. (2008). *Worldwide Prevalence of Anaemia 1993-2005: WHO Global Database on Anaemia*. Geneva: World Health Organization.

—— (2011). *Preventing Gender-biased Sex Selection: An Interagency Statement OHCHR, UNFPA, UNICEF, UN Women and WHO*. Geneva.

De Schutter, O. (2011). The World Trade Organization and the post-global food crisis agenda: putting food security first in the international trade system. Activity Report. November.

Deere, C., and others (2013). Women's land ownership and participation in agricultural decision-making: evidence from Ecuador, Ghana and Karnataka, India. Research Brief Series, No. 2. Bangalore: Indian Institute of Management.

Deininger, K., and D. Byerlee (2011). *Rising Global Interest in Farmland: Can It Yield Sustainable and Equitable Benefits?* Washington, D.C.: World Bank.

Demeke, M., and others (2012). Stabilizing price incentives for staple grain producers in the context of broader agricultural policies: debates and country experiences. ESA Working Paper, No. 12-05. Rome: Food and Agriculture Organization of the United Nations.

Doss, C. (2011). If women hold up half the sky, how much of the world's food do they produce? ESA Working Paper No. 11-04. Rome: Food and Agriculture Organization of the United Nations.

Doss, C., and others (2011). The gender asset and wealth gaps: evidence from Ecuador, Ghana, and Karnataka, India. Bangalore: Indian Institute of Management.

Doyle, T. (2005). *Environmental Movements in Minority and Majority Worlds: A Global Perspective*. New Brunswick, New Jersey: Rutgers University Press.

Doyle, T., and S. Chaturvedi (2011). Climate refugees and security: conceptualizations, categories and contestations. In The *Oxford Handbook of Climate Change and Society*, J. Dryzek, R. Norgaard and D. Schlosberg, eds. Oxford: Oxford University Press.

Dressler, W., and others (2010). From hope to crisis and back? A critical history of the global CBNRM narrative. *Environmental Conservation*, vol. 37, No. 1, pp. 5-15.

Drèze, J., and A. Sen (1991). *Hunger and Public Action*. Oxford: Oxford University Press.

Dryzek, J. S. (1997). *The Politics of the Earth: Environmental Discourses*. Oxford: Oxford University Press.

Dyson, T. (2010). *Population and Development: The Demographic Transition*. London: Zed Books.

Elson, D. (1996). Gender-aware analysis and development economics. In *The Political Economy of Development and Underdevelopment*, 6th ed., K. P. Jameson and C. K. Wilber, eds. New York: McGraw-Hill.

—— (1998). The economic, the political and the domestic: businesses, States, and households in the organisation of production. *New Political Economy*, vol. 3, No. 2, pp. 189-208.

—— (2002). Gender justice, human rights, and neo-liberal economic policies. In *Gender Justice, Development, and Rights*, M. Molyneux and S. Razavi, eds. Oxford: Oxford University Press.

—— (2011). Economics for a post-crisis world: putting social justice first. In H*arvesting Feminist Kowledge for Public Policy*, D. Jain and D. Elson, eds. New Delhi: Sage Publications India.

—— (2014). Redressing socio-economic disadvantage: women's economic and social rights and economic policy. Background paper prepared for the United Nations Entity for Gender Equality and the Empowerment of Women 2015 report on progress of the world's women. New York.

England, P., M. Budig and N. Folbre (2002). Wages of virtue: the relative pay of care work. *Social Problems*, vol. 49, No. 4, pp. 455-473.

European Institute for Gender Equality (2012). *Review of the Implementation in the EU of Area K of the Beijing Platform for Action: Women and the Environment – Gender Equality and Climate Change*. Luxembourg: Publications Office of the European Union.

Evans, P. (1995). *Embedded Autonomy: States and Industrial Transformation*. Princeton, New Jersey: Princeton University Press.

Fairhead, J. (2001). International dimensions of conflict over natural and environmental resources. In *Violent Environments*, N. L. Peluso and M. Watts, eds. Ithaca, New York: Cornell University Press.

Fairhead, J., and M. Leach (1996). *Misreading the African Landscape: Society and Ecology in a Forest-Savanna Mosaic*. Cambridge: Cambridge University Press.

Fairhead, J., M. Leach and I. Scoones (2012). Green grabbing: a new appropriation of nature? *Journal of Peasant Studies*, vol. 39, No. 2, pp. 237-261.

Feng, W., Y. Cai and B. Gu. (2013). *Population, policy and politics: how will history judge China's one-child policy? Population and Development Review*, vol. 38, Suppl. 1, pp. 115-129.

Fieldman, G. (2011). Neoliberalism, the production of vulnerability and the hobbled state: systemic barriers to climate adaptation. *Climate and Development*, vol. 3, No. 2, pp. 159-174.

Fine, B. (2012). Financialization and social policy. In *The Global Crisis and Transformative Social Change*, P. Utting, S. Razavi and R. Varghese Buchholz, eds. Basingstoke, United Kingdom: Palgrave Macmillan.

Fischer, A. M. (2014). The social value of employment and the redistributive imperative for development. Occasional Paper. New York: United Nations Development Programme, Human Development Report Office.

Fischer-Kowalski, M., and others. (2011). *Decoupling Natural Resource Use and Environmental Impacts from Economic Growth: A Report of the Working Group on Decoupling to the International Resource Panel*. United Nations Environment Programme.

Fisher, J. (2006). For her, it's the big issue: putting women at the centre of water supply, sanitation and hygiene. Evidence Report. Geneva: Water Supply and Sanitation Collaborative Council.

Folbre, N. (1994). *Who Pays for the Kids? Gender and the Structures of Constraint*. New York: Routledge.

—— (2001). *The Invisible Heart: Economics and Family Values*. New York: New Press.

—— (2006). Demanding quality: worker/consumer coalitions and "high road" strategies in the care sector. *Politics and Society*, vol. 34, No. 1, pp. 11-33.

Folke, C., and others (2011). Reconnecting to the Biosphere. *Ambio*, vol. 40, No. 7, pp. 719-738.

Food and Agriculture Organization of the United Nations (2006). *The Double Burden of Malnutrition: Case Studies from Six Developing Countries*. FAO Food and Nutrition Paper 84. Rome.

—— (2011). *The State of Food and Agriculture 2010-2011: Women in Agriculture — Closing the Gender Gap for Development*. Rome.

—— (2012). *Voluntary Guidelines on the Responsible Governance of Tenure of Land, Fisheries and Forests in the Context of National Food Security*. Rome.

—— (2013a). Food security indicators. Available from www.fao.org/economic/ ess/ess-fs/ess-fadata/en/#.U4yStPldXy0. (Accessed 2 June 2014).

—— (2013b). The State of Food and Agriculture 2013: *Food Systems for Better Nutrition*. Rome.

—— (2013c). The State of Food Insecurity in the World: The Multiple Dimensions of Food Security. Rome.

Food and Agriculture Organization of the United Nations, International Fund for Agricultural Development and International Labour Office. (2010). *Gender Dimensions of Agricultural and Rural Employment: Differentiated Pathways Out of Poverty — Status, Trends, Gaps*. Rome.

Fukuda-Parr, S., J. Heintz and S. Seguino. (2013). Critical perspectives on financial and economic crises: heterodox macroeconomics meets feminist economics. *Feminist Economics*, vol. 19, No. 3, pp. 4-31.

Fullerton, D., N. Bruce and S. B. Gordon. (2008). Indoor air pollution from biomass fuel smoke is a major health concern in the developing world. *Transactions of the Royal Society of Tropical Medicine and Hygiene*, vol. 102, No. 9, pp. 843 851.

Galbraith, J. K. (2012). Inequality and Instability: *A Study of the World Economy Just Before the Great Crisis*. New York: Oxford University Press.

Gereffi, G. (2014). Global value chains in a post-Washington Consensus world. *Review of International Political Economy*, vol. 21, No. 1, pp. 9-37.

Ghosh, J. (2010). The unnatural coupling: food and global finance. *Journal of Agrarian Change*, vol. 10, No. 1, pp. 72-86.

—— (2011). Cash transfers as the silver bullet for poverty reduction: a sceptical note. *Economic and Political Weekly*, vol. 46, No. 21, pp. 67-71.

Gillespie, S., J. Harris and S. Kadiyala (2012). The agriculture-nutrition disconnect in India: what do we know? IFPRI Discussion Paper 1187. International Food Policy Research Institute.

Global Alliance for Clean Cookstoves. (2013). *Scaling Adoption of Clean Cooking Solutions through Women's Empowerment: A Resource Guide.*

Gough, I. (2011). *Climate Change, Double Injustice and Social Policy: A Case Study of the United Kingdom.* Occasional Paper No. 1. Geneva: United Nations Research Institute for Social Development.

GRAIN. (2008). Seized: the 2008 landgrab for food and financial security. GRAIN Briefing. Barcelona.

Greenhalgh, S. (2005). *Globalization and population governance in China. In Global Assemblages: Technology, Politics, and Ethics as Anthropological Problems*, Aihwa Ong and Stephen J. Collier, eds. Malden, Massachusetts: Blackwell Publishing.

Grown, C., D. Elson and N. Cagatay. (2000). Introduction. Special issue: growth, trade, finance, and gender inequality. *World Development*, vol. 28, No. 7, pp. 1145-1156.

Guerrero, N. M., and A. Stock. (2012). Green economy from a gender perspective. Policy paper.

Guruswamy, L. (2011). Energy poverty. *Annual Review of Environment and Resources*, vol. 36, pp. 139-161.

Haddad, L. J., J. Hoddinott and H. Alderman, eds. (1997). Intrahousehold Resource Allocation in Developing Countries: Models, Methods, and Policy. Baltimore: Johns Hopkins University Press.

Hammerton, S., ed. (2013). *Decent work for domestic workers: Toward the ratification of ILO Convention 189 in Kenya, Namibia, Zambia and Zimbabwe.* Brussels: Solidar and International Federation of Workers' Education Associations.

Hammouya, M. (1999). *Statistics on Public Sector Employment: Methodology, Structures and Trends.* Working Paper SAP 2.85/WP.144. Geneva: International Labour Office.

Harcourt, W., ed. (2012). *Women Reclaiming Sustainable Livelihoods: Spaces Lost, Spaces Gained.* Basingstoke, United Kingdom: Palgrave Macmillan.

Hardin, G. (1968). The tragedy of the commons. *Science,* vol. 162, No. 3859, pp. 1243-1248.

Harris, D., M. Kooy and L. Jones. (2011). *Analysing the Governance and Political Economy of Water and Sanitation Service Delivery.* Working Paper 334. London: Overseas Development Institute.

Harriss, B. (1995). The intrafamily distribution of hunger in South Asia. In *The Political Economy of Hunger: Selected Essays*, J. Drèze, A. Sen and A. Hussain, eds. Oxford: Clarendon Press.

Harriss-White, B., and N. Gooptu (2001). Mapping India's world of unorganized labour. *Socialist Register,* vol. 37.

Hartmann, B. (1995). *Reproductive Rights and Wrongs: The Global Politics of Population Control.* Boston: South End Press.

—— (2010). Rethinking the role of population in human security. In *Global Environmental Change and Human Security*, R. A. Matthew and others, eds. Cambridge, Massachusetts: MIT Press.

Heintz, J. (2006). Low-wage manufacturing and global commodity chains: a model in the unequal exchange tradition. *Cambridge Journal of Economics*, vol. 30, No. 4, pp. 507-520.

Hernández Castillo, R. A. (2002). National law and indigenous customary law: the struggle for justice of indigenous women in Chiapas, Mexico. In *Gender Justice, Development, and Rights*, M. Molyneux and S. Razavi, eds. Oxford: Oxford University Press.

Herren, H., and others. (2012). *Green Jobs for a Revitalized Food and Agriculture Sector.* Rome: Food and Agriculture Organization of the United Nations.

Hesketh, T., L. Lu and Z. Wei Xing. (2005). The effect of China's one-child family policy after 25 years. *New England Journal of Medicine*, vol. 353, No. 11, pp. 1171-1176.

Hickling, S., and J. Bevan. (2010). Scaling up CLTS in sub-Saharan Africa. *Participatory Learning and Action*, vol. 61, pp. 51-62.

High-level Panel of Experts on Food Security and Nutrition. (2011). *Price Volatility and Food Security: A Report by the High Level Panel of Experts on Food Security and Nutrition of the Committee on World Food Security.* Rome.

—— (2012). *Food Security and Climate Change: A Report by the High Level Panel of Experts on Food Security and Nutrition of the Committee on World Food Security.* Rome.

Hildyard, N. (2010). "Scarcity" as political strategy: reflections on three hanging children. In *The Limits to Scarcity: Contesting the Politics of Allocation*, L. Mehta, ed. London: Earthscan.

Hoang, D., and B. Jones. (2012). Why do corporate codes of conduct fail? Women workers and clothing supply chains in Vietnam. *Global Social Policy*, vol. 12, No. 1, pp. 67-85.

Hoddinott, J. (1999). Operationalizing household food security in development projects: an introduction. Technical Guide No. 1. Washington, D.C.: International Food Policy Research Institute.

Hodgson, D. (1983). Demography as social science and policy science. *Population and Development Review*, vol. 9, No. 1, pp. 1-34.

Hossain, N., R. King and A. Kelbert. (2013). *Squeezed: Life in a Time of Food Price Volatility, Year 1 Results*. Oxford: Institute of Development Studies and Oxfam International.

House, S., T. Mahon and S. Cavill. (2012). *Menstrual Hygiene Matters: A Resource for Improving Menstrual Hygiene Around the World*. WaterAid.

Hutton, G., and J. Bartram (2008) Global costs of attaining the Millennium Development Goal for water supply and sanitation. *Bulletin of the World Health Organiza*tion, vol. 86, pp. 13-19.

Hutton, G., L. Haller and J. Bartram. (2007). Global cost-benefit analysis of water supply and sanitation interventions. *Journal of Water and Health*, vol. 5, No. 4, pp. 481-502.

India, Ministry of Water Resources. (2012). National Water Policy 2012.

Intergovernmental Panel on Climate Change. (2013). Summary for policymakers. In *Climate Change 2013: The Physical Science Basis — Contribution of Working Group I to the Fifth Assessment Report of the Intergovernmental Panel on Climate Change*, T. F. Stocker and others, eds. Cambridge: Cambridge University Press.

International Energy Agency. (2012). *World Energy Outlook 2012*. Paris.

International Food Policy Research Institute. (2013). Global Hunger Index database. Available from www.ifpri.org/book-8018/node/8058. Accessed 2 June 2014.

International Institute for Labour Studies. (2008). *World of Work Report 2008: Income Inequalities in the Age of Financial Globalization*. Geneva: International Labour Office.

International Labour Foundation for Sustainable Development. (2009). Green jobs and women workers: employment, equity, equality — draft report.

International Labour Organization. (2007). *ABC of Women Workers' Rights and Gender Equality*, 2nd ed. Geneva: International Labour Office.

—— (2012). *Working Towards Sustainable Development: Opportunities for Decent Work and Social Inclusion in a Green Economy*. Geneva: International Labour Office.

—— (2013). *Domestic Workers Across the World: Global and Regional Statistics and the Extent of Legal Protection*. Geneva: International Labour Office.

—— (2014). World Social Protection Report 2014/2015: Building Economic Recovery, Inclusive Development and Social Justice. Geneva: International Labour Office.

International Social Science Council, and United Nations Educational, Scientific and Cultural Organization. (2013). *World Social Science Report 2013: Changing Global Environments*. Paris: OECD Publishing and UNESCO Publishing.

Jackson, C. (1993). Doing what comes naturally? Women and environment in development. *World Development,* vol. 21, No. 12, pp. 1947-1963.

Jackson, T. (2011). Prosperity without Growth: Economics for a Finite Planet. London: Earthscan.

Jacobs, M. (2013). Green growth. In *The Handbook of Global Climate and Environmental Policy*, R. Falkner, ed. Oxford: Wiley-Blackwell.

Jacobs, S. (2010). *Gender and Agrarian Reforms*. London: Routledge.

Jacobson, A. (2007). Connective power: solar electrification and social change in Kenya. *World Development*, vol. 35, No. 1, pp. 144-162.

Johnsson-Latham, G. (2007). A *Study on Gender Equality as a Prerequisite for Sustainable Development*. Stockholm: Ministry of the Environment, Environment Advisory Council.

Kabeer, N. (2005). Gender inequality and women's empowerment: a critical analysis of the third Millennium Development Goal 1. *Gender and Development,* vol. 13, No. 1, pp. 13-24.

—— (2007). Marriage, motherhood and masculinity in the global economy: reconfigurations of personal and economic life. IDS Working Paper, No. 290. Brighton: Institute of Development Studies.

Kabeer, N., and L. Natali. (2013). Gender quality and economic growth: is there a win-win? IDS Working Paper, No. 417. Brighton: Institute of Development Studies.

Kar, K., and R. Chambers. (2008). *Handbook on Community-Led Total Sanitation*. London: Plan UK; Brighton: Institute of Development Studies.

Khan, A. (2014). Paid work as a pathway of empowerment: Pakistan's Lady Health Worker Programme. In *Feminisms, Empowerment and Development: Changing Women's Lives*, A. Cornwall and J. Edwards, eds. London: Zed Books.

King Dejardin, A. (2009). Gender (In)equality, *Globalization and Governance*. Working Paper No. 92. Geneva: International Labour Office.

Lam, N. L., and others. (2012). Household light makes global heat: high black carbon emissions from kerosene wick lamps. *Environmental Science and Technology,* vol. 46, No. 24, pp. 13531-13538.

Leach, M. (1992). Gender and the environment: traps and opportunities. *Development in Practice*, vol. 2, No. 1, pp. 12-22.

Leach, M., R. Mearns and I. Scoones. (1999). Environmental entitlements: dynamics and institutions in community-based natural resource management. *World Development*, vol. 27, No. 2, pp. 225-247.

Lee, C. M., and others. (2013). Assessing the climate impacts of cookstove projects: issues in emissions accounting. Working Paper No. 2013-01. Stockholm Environment Institute.

Lee, Ching Kwan. (2005). *Livelihood Struggles and Market Reform: (Un)making Chinese Labour after State Socialism*. Occasional Paper No. 2. Geneva: United Nations Research Institute for Social Development.

Levien, M. (2012). The land question: special economic zones and the political economy of dispossession in India. *Journal of Peasant Studies*, vol. 39, Nos. 3-4, pp. 933-969.

—— (2014). Gender and land dispossession: a comparative survey. Background paper prepared for the United Nations Entity for Gender Equality and the Empowerment of Women. New York.

Li, T. M. (2011). Centering labour in the land grab debate. *Journal of Peasant Studies*, vol. 38, No. 2, pp. 281-298.

Longhurst, R. (1988). Cash crops, household food security and nutrition. *IDS Bulletin*, vol. 19, No. 2, pp. 28-36.

Lund, F. (2010). Hierarchies of care work in South Africa: nurses, social workers, and home-based care workers. *International Labour Review*, vol. 149, No. 4, pp. 495-510.

Martínez-Alier, J. (2002). *The Environmentalism of the Poor: A Study of Ecological Conflicts and Valuation*. Cheltenham: Edward Elgar.

May, A., and G. Summerfield. (2012). Creating a space where gender matters: Elinor Ostrom (1933-2012) talks with Ann Mari May and Gale Summerfield. *Feminist Economics*, vol. 18, No. 4, pp. 25-37.

McAfee, K. (2012). The contradictory logic of global ecosystem services markets. *Development and Change*, vol. 43, No. 1, pp. 105-131.

McMahon, S., and others. (2011). "The girl with her period is the one to hang her head": reflections on menstrual management among schoolgirls in rural Kenya. *BMC International Health and Human Rights*, vol. 11.

McMichael, P. (2009). Food sovereignty, social reproduction and the agrarian question. In *Peasants and Globalization: Political Economy, Rural Transformation and the Agrarian Question*, A. H. Akram-Lodhi and C. Kay, eds. London: Routledge.

Meadows, D., and others. (1972). *The Limits to Growth: A Report to the Club of Rome's Project on the Predicament of Mankind*. New York: Universe Books.

Mehta, L., and S. Movik, eds. (2011). *Shit Matters: The Potential of Community-led Total Sanitation*. Rugby, Warwickshire: Practical Action Publishing.

Mehta, L., G. J. Veldwisch and J. Franco. (2012). Water grabbing? Focus on the (re)appropriation of finite water resources. *Water Alternatives,* vol. 5, No. 2, pp. 193-207.

Mellor, M. (2009). Ecofeminist political economy and the politics of money. In *Eco Sufficiency and Global Justice: Women Write Political Ecology*, A. Salleh, ed. London: Pluto Press.

Miah, M. D., and others. (2010). Rural household energy consumption pattern in the disregarded villages of Bangladesh. *Energy Policy*, vol. 38, No. 2, pp. 997 1003.

Millennium Ecosystem Assessment. (2005). *Ecosystems and Human Well-being: Synthesis*. Washington, D.C.: Island Press.

Minns, R., and S. Sexton. (2006). Too many grannies? Private pensions, corporate welfare and growing insecurity. The Corner House Briefing No. 35. Sturminster Newton, Dorset: The Corner House.

Mkandawire, T. (2005). Targeting and universalism in poverty reduction. Social Policy and Development Programme Paper, No. 23. Geneva: United Nations Research Institute for Social Development.

Muro, M., and others. (2011). *Sizing the clean economy. A national and regional green jobs assessment.* Washington, D.C.: Brookings Institution, Metropolitan Policy Program.

Murtaugh, P. A., and M. G. Schlax. (2009). Reproduction and the carbon legacies of individuals. *Global Environmental Change*, vol. 19, No. 1, pp. 14-20.

Myers, N., and J. Kent (1995). *Environmental Exodus: An Emergent Crisis in the Global Arena.* Washington, D.C.: Climate Institute.

Natural Capital Committee. (2013). The state of natural capital: towards a framework for measurement and valuation.

Nelson, G. C., and others. (2009). *Climate Change: Impact on Agriculture and Costs of Adaptation.* Washington, D.C.: International Food Policy Research Institute.

Nelson, K., and A. Murray. (2008). Sanitation for unserved populations: technologies, implementation challenges, and opportunities. *Annual Review of Environment and Resources*, vol. 33, pp. 119-151.

Neumayer, E., and T. Plümper. (2007). The gendered nature of natural disasters: the impact of catastrophic events on the gender gap in life expectancy, 1981-2002. *Annals of the Association of American Geographers*, vol. 97, No. 3, pp. 551 566.

Nussbaum, M. (2000). *Women and Human Development: The Capabilities Approach.* Cambridge: Cambridge University Press.

Odum, E. (1953). *The Fundamentals of Ecology.* Philadelphia: W. B. Saunders.

O'Neill, B. C., and others. (2010). Global demographic trends and future carbon emissions. *Proceedings of the National Academy of Sciences of the United States of America*, vol. 107, No. 41, pp. 17521-17526.

Oostendorp, R. H. (2009). Globalization and the gender wage gap. *World Bank Economic Review*, vol. 23, No. 1, pp. 141-161.

Organization for Economic Cooperation and Development. (2012). *Closing the Gender Gap: Act Now.* Paris: OECD Publishing.

Ortiz, I., and M. Cummins. (2013). The age of austerity: a review of public expenditures and adjustment measures in 181 countries. Working paper. New York: Initiative for Policy Dialogue; Geneva: South Centre.

Ostrom, E. (2000). Collective action and the evolution of social norms. *Journal of Economic Perspectives*, vol. 14, No. 3, pp. 137-158.

Otzelberger, A. (2011). Gender-responsive strategies on climate change: recent progress and ways forward for donors. Brighton: Institute of Development Studies, BRIDGE.

Pachauri, S., and others. (2012). Energy access for development. In *Global Energy Assessment: Toward a Sustainable Future*, T. B. Johansson and others, eds. Cambridge: Cambridge University Press; Laxenburg, Austria: International Institute for Applied Systems Analysis.

Peng, I. (2012). The boss, the worker, his wife and no babies: South Korean political and social economy of care in a context of institutional rigidities. In *Global Variations in the Political and Social Economy of Care: Worlds Apart*, S. Razavi and S. Staab, eds. New York: Routledge.

Pereira, M. G., and others. (2011). Evaluation of the impact of access to electricity: a comparative analysis of South Africa, China, India and Brazil. *Renewable and Sustainable Energy Reviews*, vol. 15, No. 3, pp. 1427-1441.

Quisumbing, A., and others (2008). Helping women respond to the global food price crisis. IFPRI Policy Brief, No. 7, Washington, D.C. International Food Policy Research Institute.

Raupach, M. R., and others. (2007). Global and regional drivers of accelerating CO2 emissions. *Proceedings of the National Academy of Sciences of the United States of America*, vol. 104, No. 24, pp. 10288-10293.

Raworth, K. (2012). A safe and just space for humanity: Can we live within the doughnut? Oxfam Discussion Paper. Oxford: Oxfam International.

Ray, I. (2007). Women, water and development. *Annual Review of Environment and Resources*, vol. 32, pp. 421-449.

Razavi, S. (2007). The political and social economy of care in a development context: conceptual issues, research questions and policy options. Gender and Development Programme Paper, No. 3. Geneva: United Nations Research Institute for Social Development.

—— (2009). Engendering the political economy of agrarian change. *Journal of Peasant Studies*, vol. 36, No. 1, pp. 197-227.

Razavi, S., and others. (2012). Gendered impacts of globalization: employment and social protection. Research and Policy Brief, No. 13. Geneva: United Nations Research Institute for Social Development.

Razavi, S., and S. Hassim, eds. (2006). *Gender and Social Policy in a Global Context: Uncovering the Gendered Structure of "the Social"*. Basingstoke, United Kingdom: Palgrave Macmillan.

Razavi, S., and S. Staab. (2010). Underpaid and overworked: a cross-national perspective on care workers. *International Labour Review*, vol. 149, No. 4, pp. 407-422.

Rival, L. (2012). *Sustainable Development Through Policy Integration in Latin America: A Comparative Approach*. Occasional Paper No. 7. Geneva: United Nations Research Institute for Social Development.

Robertson, T. (2012). *The Malthusian Movement: Global Population Growth and the Birth of American Environmentalism*. New Brunswick, New Jersey: Rutgers University Press.

Rocheleau M., D. (1988). *Gender, resource management and the rural landscape: implications for agroforestry and farming systems research. In Gender Issues in Farming Systems Research and Extension*, S. V. Poats, M. Schmink and A. Spring, eds. Boulder: Westview Press.

Rockström, J. W., and others (2009). Planetary boundaries: exploring the safe operating space for humanity. *Ecology and Society*, vol. 14, No. 2.

Rodda, A. (1991). *Women and the Environment*. London: Zed Books.

Roe, E. M. (1995). Except-Africa: postscript to a special section on development narratives. *World Development*, vol. 23, No. 6, pp. 1065-1069.

Rukuni, S. (2010). Challenging mindsets: CLTS and government policy in Zimbabwe. *Participatory Learning and Action,* vol. 61, pp. 141-148.

Saith, A. (2011). Inequality, imbalance, instability: reflections on a structural crisis. *Development and Change*, vol. 42, No. 1, pp. 70-86.

Saith, R., and B. Harriss-White (1999). The gender sensitivity of well-being indicators. *Development and Change*, vol. 30, No. 3, pp. 465-497.

Samson, M., ed. (2009). *Refusing to Be Cast Aside: Waste Pickers Organising Around the World*. Cambridge, Massachusetts: Women in Informal Employment: Globalizing and Organizing.

Satterthwaite, D. (2009). The implications of population growth and urbanization for climate change. *Environment and Urbanization*, vol. 21, No. 2, pp. 545 567.

Satterthwaite, D., D. Mitlin and S. Patel (2011). Engaging with the urban poor and their organizations for poverty reduction and urban governance. Issues paper. New York: United Nations Development Programme.

Say, L., and others (2014). Global causes of maternal death: a WHO systematic analysis. *The Lancet Global Health*, vol. 2, no. 6, pp. e323-e333.

Sayre, N. F. (2008). The genesis, history and limits of carrying capacity. *Annals of the Association of American Geographers*, vol. 98, No. 1, pp. 120-134.

Schalatek, L. (2013). The post-2015 framework: merging care and green economy approaches to finance gender-equitable sustainable development. Washington, D.C.: Heinrich Böll Stiftung.

Seguino, S. (2000). Gender inequality and economic growth: a cross-country analysis. *World Development*, vol. 28, No. 7, pp. 1211-1230.

—— (2010). Gender, distribution, and balance of payments constrained growth in developing countries. *Review of Political Economy*, vol. 22, No. 3, pp. 373 404.

Seguino, S., and C. Grown. (2006). Gender equity and globalization: macroeconomic policy for developing countries. *Journal of International Development*, vol. 18, No. 8, pp. 1081-1104.

Sen, A. (1982). *Poverty and Famines: An Essay on Entitlement and Deprivation*. Oxford: Oxford University Press.

—— (1985). Well-being, agency and freedom: the Dewey Lectures 1984. *Journal of Philosophy*, vol. 82, No. 4, pp. 169-221.

—— (1990). More than 100 million women are missing. *New York Review of Books*, vol. 37, No. 20 (20 December).

—— (1999). *Development as Freedom*. New York: Knopf.

Sen, G., and A. Nayar. (2013). Population, environment and human rights: a paradigm in the making. In *Powerful Synergies: Gender Equality, Economic Development and Environmental Sustainability*, B. Cela, I. Dankelman and J. Stern, eds. New York: United Nations Development Programme.

Sepúlveda, M., and C. Nyst. (2012). *The Human Rights Approach to Social Protection.* Helsinki: Ministry for Foreign Affairs of Finland.

Shah, S. P., and others. (2013). Improving quality of life with new menstrual hygiene practices among adolescent tribal girls in rural Gujarat, India. *Reproductive Health Matters,* vol. 21, No. 41, pp. 205-213.

Sidner, S. (2011). Solar panels power profit in Bangladesh. CNN.com, 12 April. Accessed 25 January 2014. Available from http://edition.cnn.com/2011/ BUSINESS/04/11/bangladesh.solar.power.kalihati. Sinton, J. E., and others (2004). An assessment of programs to promote improved household stoves in China. *Energy for Sustainable Development,* vol. 8, No. 3, pp. 33-52.

Skinner, E. (2011). *Gender and Climate Change: Overview Report.* BRIDGE Cutting Edge Pack Series. Brighton: Institute of Development Studies.

Sovacool, B. K. (2012). The political economy of energy poverty: a review of key challenges. *Energy for Sustainable Development,* vol. 16, No. 3, pp. 272-282.

Statistics South Africa. (2013). *General Household Survey 2012.* Pretoria.

Stern, N. (2006). What is the economics of climate change? *World Economics,* vol. 7, No. 2.

Stiglitz, J. E. (2012). The Price of Inequality: *How Today's Divided Society Endangers Our Future.* New York: W. W. Norton and Company.

Stirling, A. (1998). Risk at a turning point? *Journal of Risk Research,* vol. 1, No. 2, pp. 97-109.

Stockhammer, E. (2013). *Why Have Wage Shares Fallen? A Panel Analysis of the Determinants of Functional Income Distribution.* Conditions of Work and Employment Series No. 35, Geneva: International Labour Office.

Strietska-Ilina, O., and others. (2011). *Skills for Green Jobs: A Global View — Synthesis Report Based on 21 Country Studies.* Geneva: International Labour Office.

Szreter, S. (1993). The idea of demographic transition and the study of fertility change: a critical intellectual history. *Population and Development Review,* vol. 19, No. 4, pp. 659-701.

Tiba, Z. (2011). Targeting the most vulnerable: implementing input subsidies. In *Safeguarding Food Security in Volatile Markets,* A. Prakash, ed. Rome: Food and Agriculture Organization of the United Nations.

Tomlinson, I. (2013). Doubling food production to feed the 9 billion: a critical perspective on a key discourse of food security in the UK. *Journal of Rural Studies,* vol. 29, pp. 81-90.

United Nations. (1975). *Report of the World Food Conference,* Rome 5-16 November 1974. Sales No. E.75.II.A.3.

—— (1999). *The World at Six Billion.* ESA/P/WP.154.

—— (2001). *World Population Prospects: The 2000 Revision,* vol. I, *Comprehensive Tables,* vol. II, *Sex and Age,* vol. III, *Analytical Report.* Sales No. E.91.XIII.8, E.01.XIII.9 and E.01.XIII.20.

—— (2002). *Abortion Policies: A Global Review,* vol. I, *Afghanistan to France,* vol. II, *Gabon to Norway* and vol. III, *Oman to Zimbabwe.* Sales Nos. E.01.XIII.10, E.01.XIII.18 and E.02.XIII.5.

—— (2009). *World Survey on the Role of Women in Development: Women's Control over Economic Resources and Access to Financial Resources, including Microfinance.* Sales No. E.09.IV.7.

—— (2010). *The World's Women: Trends and Statistics.* Sales No. E.10.XVII.11.

—— (2013a). *The Millennium Development Goals Report.* Sales No. E.13.I.9.

—— (2013b). *Report on the World Social Situation 2013: Inequality Matters.* Sales No. E.13.IV.2.

—— (2013c). *World Population Ageing 2013.* Sales No. E.14.XIII.6.

—— (2013d). *World Population Prospects: The 2012 Revision — Key Findings and Advance Tables.* Working Paper No. ESA/P/WP.227.

United Nations Children's Fund. (2008). *The State of the World's Children 2009: Maternal and Newborn Health.* Sales No. E.09.XX.1.

—— (2013). *Improving Child Nutrition: The Achievable Imperative for Global Progress.* Sales No. E.13.XX.4.

United Nations Children's Fund, and Central Institute for Fiscal Studies (ICEFI). (2011). Protecting the new harvest: an analysis of the cost of eradicating hunger in Guatemala 2012-2021. Bulletin, No. 4. Guatemala.

United Nations Conference on Trade and Development. (2010). *Trade and Development Report 2010: Employment, Globalization and Development.* Sales No. E.10.II.D.3.

—— (2013a). *Trade and Development Report 2013: Adjusting to the Changing Dynamics of the World Economy.* Sales No. E.13. II.D.3.

—— (2013b). *World Investment Report 2013: Global Value Chains — Investment and Trade for Development.* Sales No. E.13. II.D.5.

United Nations Development Programme. (1995). *Human Development Report 1995: Gender and Human Development.* New York: Oxford University Press.

—— (2006). *Human Development Report 2006: Beyond Scarcity — Power, Poverty and the Global Water Crisis.* Basingstoke, United Kingdom: Palgrave Macmillan.

—— (2011). *Human Development Report 2011: Sustainability and Equity — A Better Future for All.* Basingstoke, United Kingdom: Palgrave Macmillan.

—— (2013a). *Human Development Report 2013: The Rise of the South — Human Progress in a Diverse World.* New York.

—— (2013b). *Humanity Divided: Confronting Inequality in Developing Countries.* New York.

United Nations Entity for Gender Equality and the Empowerment of Women and Mary Robinson Foundation-Climate Justice. (2013). The full view: advancing the goal of gender balance in multilateral and intergovernmental processes. New York and Dublin.

United Nations Environment Programme. (2009). Global green new deal: policy brief. Nairobi.

—— (2011). *Towards a Green Economy: Pathways to Sustainable Development and Poverty Eradication* — A Synthesis for Policy Makers. Nairobi.

United Nations Environment Programme, and others. (2008). *Green Jobs: Towards Decent Work in a Sustainable, Low Carbon World.* Nairobi: United Nations Environment Programme.

United Nations International Strategy for Disaster Reduction (secretariat). (2009). *Global Assessment Report on Disaster Risk Reduction.* Geneva. United Nations Entity for Gender Equality and the Empowerment of Women. (2014). Gender equality and the global economic crisis. Research paper. New York.

United Nations Millennium Project, Task Force on Hunger (2005). Halving Hunger: It Can Be Done. London: Earthscan.

United Nations Office for Disaster Risk Reduction (2009). Global Assessment Report on Disaster Risk Reduction. Geneva.

United Nations Research Institute for Social Development. (2010). *Combating Poverty and Inequality: Structural Change, Social Policy and Politics.* Sales No. E.10.III.Y.1.

—— (2012a). Inequalities and the post-2015 development agenda. Research and Policy Brief, No. 15. Geneva.

—— (2012b). Social dimensions of green economy. Research and Policy Brief, No. 12. Geneva.

Unmüßig, B. (2014). On the value of nature: the merits and perils of a new economy of nature. Berlin: Heinrich Böll Stiftung.

Unmüßig, B., W. Sachs, and T. Fatheuer (2012). *Critique of the Green Economy: Toward Social and Environmental Equity.* Publication Series on Ecology, No. 22, Berlin: Heinrich Böll Stiftung.

Unterhalter, E. (2013). The MDGs, girls' education and gender equality. Paper prepared for the expert group meeting on structural and policy constraints in achieving the Millennium Development Goals for women and girls. Mexico City: October.

Urdal, H. (2012). A clash of generations? Youth bulges and political violence. Expert Paper, No. 2012/1. New York: Department of Economic and Social Affairs, Population Division.

Vanek, J., and others. (forthcoming). *Statistics on the Informal Economy: Definitions, Regional Estimates and Challenges.* WIEGO Working Paper (Statistics), No. 2. Cambridge, Massachusetts: Women in Informal Employment: Globalizing and Organizing.

Vaughan, G., ed. (2007). *Women and the Gift Economy: A Radically Different Worldview is Possible.* Toronto: Inanna Publications and Education.

Vizard, P., S. Fukuda-Parr and D. Elson. (2011). Introduction: the capability approach and human rights. *Journal of Human Development and Capabilities*, vol. 12, No. 1, pp. 1-22.

Vogt, W. (1948). *Road to Survival.* New York: W. Sloane Associates.

Von Braun, J. (2014). Aiming for food and nutrition security in a changed global context: strategy to end hunger. In *Alternative Development Strategies in the Post-2015* Era, J. A. Alonso, G. A. Cornia and R. Vos, eds. New York and London: Bloomsbury Academic.

Von Grebmer, K., and others. (2013). *2013 Global Hunger Index: The Challenge of Hunger — Building Resilience to Achieve Food and Nutrition Security*. Bonn: Welthungerhilfe; Washington D.C.: International Food Policy Research Institute; Dublin: Concern Worldwide.

White, J., and B. White. (2012). Gendered experiences of dispossession: oil palm expansion in a Dayak Hibun community in West Kalimantan. *Journal of Peasant Studies*, vol. 39, Nos. 3-4, pp. 995-1016.

World Health Organization. (2009). *Global Health Risks: Mortality and Burden of Disease Attributable to Selected Major Risks*. Geneva.

—— (2012). *UN-Water Global Annual Assessment of Sanitation and Drinking-Water (GLAAS) 2012 Report: The Challenge of Extending and Sustaining Services*. Geneva.

World Health Organization, and United Nations Children's Fund. (2006). *Meeting the MDG Drinking-Water and Sanitation Target: The Urban and Rural Challenge of the Decade*. Geneva and New York.

—— (2012). *Progress on Drinking Water and Sanitation: 2012 Update*. Geneva and New York.

—— (2013). *Progress on Sanitation and Drinking-Water: 2013 Update*. Geneva and New York.

—— (2014). *Progress on Drinking Water and Sanitation: 2014 update*. Geneva and New York.

Wichterich, C. (2012). *The Future We Want: A Feminist Perspective*. Publication Series on Ecology, No. 21. Berlin: Heinrich Böll Stiftung.

Wider Opportunities for Women. (2012). WANTO: Women in Apprenticeship and Nontraditional Occupations Act. Fact Sheet. Washington, D.C.

Williams, G. (1995). Modernizing Malthus: the World Bank, population control and the African environment. In *Power of Development*, J. Crush, ed. London: Routledge.

Wiltshire, R. (1992). Environment and development: grassroots' women's perspectives. Barbados: Development Alternatives with Women for a New Era.

Women Organizing for Change in Agriculture and Natural Resource Management, and others. (2013). Scoping study of good practices for strengthening women's inclusion in forest and other natural resource management sectors: joint regional initiative for women's inclusion in REDD+.

Women's Major Group. (2013). *Gender Equality, Women's Rights and Women's Priorities: Recommendations for the Proposed Sustainable Development Goals (SDGs) and the Post-2015 Development Agenda*.

Wong, S. (2009). Climate change and sustainable technology: re-linking poverty, gender, and governance. *Gender and Development*, vol. 17, No. 1, pp. 95-108.

World Bank. (2003). *World Development Report 2004: Making Services Work for Poor People*. Washington, D.C.: World Bank; Oxford: Oxford University Press.

—— (2011). *Gender and Climate Change: Three Things You Should Know*. Washington, D.C.

—— (2012). *World Development Report 2012: Gender Equality and Development*. Washington, D.C.

—— (2014). *World Development Indicators 2014*. Washington, D.C.

World Commission on Dams. (2000). *Dams and Development: A New Framework for Decision-making — The Report of the World Commission on Dams*. London: Earthscan.

Wright, B. D. (2012). International grain reserves and other instruments to address volatility in grain markets. *World Bank Research Observer*, vol. 27, No. 2, pp. 222-260.

Xing, Li. (2009). Population control called key to deal. *China Daily*. Available from www.chinadaily.com.cn/china/2009-12/10/content_9151129.htm. Accessed 22 June 2014.

Yamin, A. E., and V. M. Boulanger. (2013). Embedding sexual and reproductive health and rights in a transformational development framework: lessons learned from the MDG targets and indicators. *Reproductive Health Matters*, vol. 21, No. 42, pp. 74-85.

Zhang, J., and K. R. Smith. (2007). Household air pollution from coal and biomass fuels in China: measurements, health impacts, and interventions. *Environmental Health Perspectives*, vol. 115 No. 6, pp. 848-855.

Zwarteveen, M. (1997). Water: from basic need to commodity: a discussion on gender and water rights in the context of irrigation. *World Development*, vol. 25, No. 8, pp. 1335-1349.